Belief and Evangelism

Belief and Evangelism

Douglas Vickers

WIPF & STOCK · Eugene, Oregon

BELIEF AND EVANGELISM

Copyright © 2018 Douglas Vickers. All rights reserved. Except for brief quotations in critical publications or reviews, no part of this book may be reproduced in any manner without prior written permission from the publisher. Write: Permissions, Wipf and Stock Publishers, 199 W. 8th Ave., Suite 3, Eugene, OR 97401.

Wipf & Stock
An Imprint of Wipf and Stock Publishers
199 W. 8th Ave., Suite 3
Eugene, OR 97401

www.wipfandstock.com

PAPERBACK ISBN: 978-1-5326-4894-6
HARDCOVER ISBN: 978-1-5326-4895-3
EBOOK ISBN: 978-1-5326-4896-0

Manufactured in the U.S.A.

Scriptural quotations are from the King James Version unless otherwise stated.

For
Al and Nan LaValley
with affection and gratitude
for their faithful ministry
of the word of God

Contents

Preface | ix

1. Issues and Objectives | 1
2. Does God Exist? | 11
3. The Knowledge of God | 30
4. The Triune Redemption of the Church | 47
5. Covenantal Justification | 65
6. The Covenantal Christian Life | 79
7. The Sabbath Obligation | 92
8. Oaths and the *Imago Dei* | 114
9. Conclusion | 129

Bibliography | 133

Preface

My intention in this book is to raise an important question in the life and testimony of the church at this time. I refer to the content of, and the relation between, what I shall designate as the church's evangel on the one hand and its evangelism on the other. I am speaking, as my title states, of evangelism, deliberately avoiding use of the term evangelicalism. That is because the issues that have attracted my attention appear to come to expression not only in that wide testimony of the church that has come to be referred to as evangelicalism, but also in the church in its Reformed expression.

The development and unity of the book are exhibited more fully in the first chapter. At this point it will be useful to indicate a principal issue that has motivated what follows. That has to do with the redemptive work and suffering of Christ. Bringing to emphasis what I shall refer to as the humanness of Christ and the soulish aspect and the bodily aspect of his human nature, the meaning of his sacrificial offering is not adequately stated until his suffering on the cross in soulish aspect is addressed. In that, he passed through eternal death and was victorious over it. He then moved at the time of his own choosing to his temporal death. While full recognition is maintained of the necessity and importance of Christ's shedding his blood in his vicarious sacrifice, the reference to the blood is properly to be understood as a synecdochical reference to his total redemptive offering. The theological-doctrinal importance of that relation is indicated briefly in chapter 1, and its significance for the evangelism of the church is explored more fully in chapter 4.

The chapters can most profitably be read in the order in which they appear, thereby maintaining continuity of development. But they are to some degree independent and may be read selectively. For that reason, a minimal repetition of crucial interpretative concepts appears in some places.

Preface

I am indebted for encouragement in the development of this work to the Reverend Al LaValley, and for assistance in bringing it to publication, to Ann Hopkins. This affords me the opportunity, which I embrace gladly, to say "thank you" to Ann for her invaluable assistance over many years and numerous publication ventures. I retain responsibility for errors and blemishes that remain in the book.

Chapter 1

Issues and Objectives

We live in a hurried age. The import and significance of the fact pardons the cliché of the statement and preserves it from the trite and the commonplace. Attention spans are narrowed now, it seems, and sound bites and superficialities have taken the place of hard-wrought inquiry and expanded understanding. Little time remains, it appears, for meditation and its calming or at least explanatory effects, the art of reflection has been dampened, and lives are ruled by the rush of everyday. We live in an attenuated age, in a sense a cramped and unfulfilling age.

Into this existential and all-too-human complex comes the gospel of Jesus Christ with its demand for response. Two questions project their appeal to the reflective mind: Who is Jesus Christ? And why did Jesus Christ come into the world? The answers can be put in brief. Jesus Christ was, and he continued to be, the eternal ever-blessed Second Person of the Godhead who came into the world to become Jesus Christ for the redemption of the people whom God the Father had given to him for that purpose (John 17:6, 9). But beyond that response remain two questions that trouble the church, and that disturb inquiring minds within the church. What, in the present time of uncertainties in belief and experimentation in life commitments, is the further response to two questions that emanate from what has just been said? First, what is understood as the non-negotiable content of the gospel or, as we shall refer to it, the evangel; and second, to what extent does the preaching of the church, the evangelism of its pulpit ministry, preserve the evangel? In short, what is the evangel, and are we faithful to the deposit of truth that it conveys?

In our entry to those important questions the emphasis of our studies falls on the fact that it was *Jesus* Christ with whose redemptive accomplishment we are concerned. Jesus was his human name, as was stated to Joseph who was betrothed to the virgin who would bear the child, "Thou shalt call his name JESUS; for he will save his people from their sins" (Matt 1:21). In the following chapters we intend to bring into increasing focus the humanness of Christ. We are interested, for that purpose, in the human nature of Christ. He came into the world to take a human nature into union with his divine nature in order that in that human nature, a created, finite, and temporal human nature, he might do two things. In doing so he would satisfy all the necessities relevant to the redemption of the people he set out to redeem from the estate of sin into which they had fallen. That estate followed as a result of their first parent's, Adam's, sin. As the *Westminster Shorter Catechism* puts is, "The covenant being made with Adam, not only for himself, but for his posterity, all mankind, descending from him by ordinary generation, sinned in him, and fell with him in his first transgression."[1]

First, Christ having taken to himself a "true body and a reasonable soul" yet without sin,[2] he would act as the substitute for his people by fulfilling all of the demands of the law of God that they had failed to honor. In that respect, he came to do for his people what they were obligated to do under the covenant that God had established with them but which they could not do for themselves by reason of their captivity to Satan and sin. Second, after Christ had in that way fulfilled the demands of the law from which his people had derogated, he laid down his life in payment of the penalty due to the justice of God for their having broken the law. The righteousness of God demanded first, that the law must be fulfilled and honored, and second, that the penalty for breaking the law must be paid.

With those primary data in view, the principal objective of our present studies is to remark further on the deeper implications of the reality involved in those redemptive processes. That reality resides in the fact that it was in his human nature that Jesus Christ discharged those redemptive obligations. That is to say, we shall be much concerned with what we can now refer to respectively as the *bodily aspect* of our Lord's human nature and the *soulish aspect* of that nature, with what is attributable to each, and with their respective significance in Christ's total redemptive offering. It is

---

1. *Westminster Shorter Catechism*, Question 16.
2. See ibid., Question 22.

necessary to have full regard to the relevance of both soul and body in the total complex of that redemptive accomplishment.

Our argument in those respects is motivated by the fear that in the evangelism and the pulpit ministry of the church, minimal and inadequate attention has been accorded the pressing reality and implications of what has just been said. The explanation of Christ's suffering is incomplete unless and until his suffering of human soul on the cross is addressed. In his presence in this world Jesus Christ, having assumed a *human nature*, did not thereby become a *human person*. He was and he remained a *divine person*. It is to be held that in his total activity in this world, certain actions that were directly attributable to his human nature were properly the actions of the *person* of our Lord, and similarly, those actions directly attributable to his divine nature were properly the actions of his *person*. Christ discharged his redemptive commitment, that is, in his human nature. He fulfilled the law of God in his human nature, and he died in his human nature. He could not die in his divine nature. But the apostle to the Corinthians has clarified that while his death was death in his human nature, it is nevertheless properly and profoundly necessary to state that it was the Son of God who died in that human nature. None of the authorities who were responsible for his death knew who he was. "For had they known it, they would not have crucified the Lord of Glory" (1 Cor 2:8). It was the Lord of glory who died in his human nature.

It will anticipate our further conclusions to state that for those reasons we shall refer to Christ's suffering of soul on the cross as his passing through eternal death. Christ was not, in that sacred moment, overcome by death, but he remained in control of all the processes of the onslaughts of Satan and the sword of justice of God his Father, and he conquered death and passed victoriously through it. He accomplished that by the Holy Spirit's support of his human nature. For it is said at Hebrews 9:14 that it was "through the eternal Spirit" that he "offered himself without spot to God." Our Lord had prayed to the Father who "was able to save him from death, *and was heard*" (Heb 5:7, italics added). He did not pray to be saved from dying. Indeed, at the end of his Galilean ministry he "stedfastly set his face to go to Jerusalem" for that very purpose (Luke 9:51). He prayed to be saved from death, and as has just been said, in that he was heard he was saved from death. Death did not defeat or conquer him. He conquered death. At no time was he not in control of the process of suffering of soul that was involved in those moments of dereliction.

When, then, Christ had emerged victorious over death, in what we have referred to as his passing through *eternal death* on behalf of the people he set out to redeem, and when the Father's smile of satisfaction had returned to him, he voluntarily, at his own time and choosing, laid down his human life in what we shall refer to as his *temporal death*. He committed his spirit, his human soul, to the Father. For he had said, in his discourse on his identity as the good shepherd who gives his life for his sheep, that "I lay down my life . . . No man taketh it from me, but I lay it down of myself" (John 10:17-18). We shall return expansively to those highly important relationships in the total redemptive offering of Christ.

Theological apologetics

We shall encounter in the following chapters certain aspects of theological apologetics as they bear on the principal questions under discussion. It can be asked, for example, whether it can be known, and if so how it can be known, that God exists? Is it possible to establish convincing proofs or demonstration that God exists? If God exists, is it possible to know God or, at the same time, to know what God knows? If it is granted that God exists, how, then, is a reliable relation established between the consequent knowledge of God and the offer of the gospel of salvation that the Scriptures copiously declare? For the present, therefore, it will be useful to make some brief comments on the reasons for and the scope of apologetics and its place in the theological scheme of things.

Apologetics, in short, is that part of theology that establishes a defense of the faith to which one is committed. An earlier work that served its time in the late nineteenth century was that of A. B. Bruce, titled *Apologetics, or Christianity Defensively Stated*.[3] The aspect of defense that Bruce raises, and the necessity of it, recall the advice of the apostle Peter who stated: "Be ready always to give an answer to every man that asketh you a reason for the hope that is in you with meekness and fear" (1 Pet 3:15). In general terms, an older tradition in apologetics was concerned to lay the foundation on which knowledge of God and the articulation of biblical doctrine could proceed. That God existed needed to be demonstrated before statements about God and what he might have said and done could be properly examined. Apologetic thought centered to a significant degree in what were referred to as the classical proofs of God's existence. We shall refer to those

3. Bruce, *Apologetics*.

so-called proofs in a moment, but a fuller discussion of them and of their logical and practical value will come at a later stage.

It is not necessary for our present purposes to rehearse at length all of the fashions in thought that interested the theologians as apologetic foundations developed. An indication of what was perhaps a predominant standpoint in the nineteenth century is contained in the opening sentences of the *Systematic Theology* by Charles Hodge, the distinguished occupant of the Chair in theology at Princeton Theological Seminary. Hodge sets out his viewpoint as follows: "In every science there are two factors: facts and ideas; or, facts and the mind. Science is more than knowledge. Knowledge is the persuasion of what is true on adequate evidence."[4] For Hodge, theology took its place among the sciences by its adoption of a uniform methodological procedure, the marshaling of facts and the inductive conclusion as to truth on the basis of derivation from the facts. We note the critical importance of the facts. But as we shall argue at a later point, differences of view may well exist as to what, in reality, are the facts. We shall observe that it is the meaning of the fact that gives the fact its factness. But we leave that conceivably important point for the present.

The understanding of the place and importance of "evidence," however, has remained an important part of that expression of apologetics that has become known as *evidentialism*. That scheme of thought argues inductively from collectible facts to so-called statements of truth. A prominent contemporary theological scholar who is a dedicated evidentialist is R. C. Sproul who has co-authored *Classical Apologetics*.[5] It is sufficient to say at this point that evidentialism, carrying with it the assumption of the competence of unaided reason to marshal the facts, is essentially a form of theological rationalism. That is reflected in the presence of "rational" in Sproul's full title. It in effect fails to grasp what we shall refer to as the antithesis between the natural and unregenerate mind on the one hand, and the regenerate mind on the other.

Perhaps the main elements of evidentialism as an apologetic system are clearest in the work of John Blanchard, who authored *Does God believe in atheists?*[6] On the question of the possibility of the existence of God, for example, and indeed on the possibility of knowing in general, Blanchard reaches the following conclusions: "The right approach to the subject of

---

4. Hodge, *Systematic Theology*, I:1.
5. Sproul, et al., *Classical Apologetics*, 4.
6. Blanchard, *Does God believe in atheists?*

the existence of God is to assemble and assess all the data we can and then come to a conclusion based on what we consider satisfying evidence or reasonable probabilities."[7] Blanchard continues, citing with approbation the work of Alister McGrath: "The attempt to establish primary truths on which we can build absolute knowledge has proved to be futile. As Alister McGrath points out, 'The dream of finding self-evident truths, known with total certainty, and upon which an entire system of beliefs could be erected, is now seen to be a delusion. All our knowledge about anything that really matters is a matter of probability.'"

What the evidentialist system of thought does, basing its structure, as has been seen, on the assumption of the competence of unaided human reason, is to assume that there exists what we may refer to as reason-in-general that both the regenerate and the unregenerate share. In other terms, evidentialism assumes in that way that apologetics is prior to theology. It is assumed to lay the groundwork for theology. Theological doctrine follows, in that scheme of things, after the groundwork for it, and the potential and putative validity of it, have been established by the operation of the sovereign human mind.

An alternative and, we conclude, preferred system of Christian apologetics is that known as presuppositionalism, already referred to in the title of Sproul's book which was in itself an attempt to controvert the presuppositional system. A Christian apologetic, it is argued, properly begins with the presupposition that *God is*. The rightful place of the human mind is preserved, but rather than arguing from man to God in the manner of evidentialism, presuppositionalism argues from God to man. The most articulate formulation of presuppositionalism is found in the work of Cornelius Van Til,[8] and has been discussed by numerous scholars, including notably John M. Frame, Greg L. Bahnsen and more recently K. Scott Oliphint.[9]

The spirit of Van Til's presuppositionalism is disclosed in his insightful comparison of, and differentiation between, the knowledge and epistemic capacities of the Christian and the non-believer: "Metaphysically, both parties have all things in common, while epistemologically they have nothing in common."[10] Acknowledging that the laws of logic are the same for both

---

7. Ibid., 194.

8. Van Til, *Defense of the Faith*; *Christian Theory of Knowledge*; *Common Grace*.

9. See Frame, *Cornelius Van Til*, *Apologetics*, and *History*; Bahnsen, *Van Til's Apologetic*; Oliphint, *Covenantal Apologetics*.

10. Van Til, *Common Grace*, 5.

the regenerate and the unregenerate man, Van Til insightfully draws out the difference between them: "It is either the would be autonomous man, who weighs and measures what he thinks of as brute or bare facts by the help of what he thinks of as abstract impersonal principles, or it is the believer, knowing himself to be a creature of God, who weighs and measures what he thinks of as God-created facts by what he thinks of as God-created laws."[11] Van Til is there insisting on what we referred to earlier as the antithesis between the regenerate and the unregenerate minds.

Presuppositionalism, in such ways, departs from the assumption of the autonomy of the human mind in the discovery and formulation of truth. For presuppositionalism there is no such thing as a reason-in-general that the natural unregenerate man and the Christian believer share.

It was mentioned that as part of certain apologetic systems reliance has been made on certain so-called proofs of the existence of God. They include, for example, a so-called ontological proof of God's existence, first proposed by the theologian, Anselm, at the end of the eleventh century. Its essence is stated at this point because, as will be observed in a later chapter, there is reason to conclude, as did the philosopher Immanuel Kant, that certain remaining proofs depended for their validity on the assumed competence of the ontological proof, and if the latter were shown to be invalid the proofs in general fall to the ground.

Briefly stated, the ontological proof posited that it was possible to think of a being greater than which no other being could be thought. That being was designated God. Many subsequent writers properly pointed out that a fallacy existed in the "proof" because of the hidden assumption that existence was a necessary predicate. It was argued, that is, that the being who was assumed in the "proof" could not be predicated necessarily to exist. That damaging response to the proof has been repeated many times in the subsequent literature, but it has continued to maintain force in some circles.

Fuller reference will be made in a following chapter to certain other so-called proofs. The cosmological proof traces back to a first cause of what exists. The argument from design attributes unmistakable evidences of design in the empirical state of affairs to a designer who is designated God. A teleological proof argued that God was necessary to account for the elements of purposiveness that were clearly observable.

---

11. Ibid., 44.

The way ahead

Our objective in what lies ahead is to address certain aspects of the redemption of the church and to exhibit some important features of the church's existence and obligations. That objective will be realized in four groupings of chapters. First, two chapters will address the question of the existence and knowability of God who has provided and brought to effect the redemption of the church; second, one chapter will bring together the central aspects of the triune redemption of the church, having regard principally to the redemptive suffering of Christ; third, two chapters will focus on the covenantal characteristics of the redemptive work of Christ and of the Christian life within the church; fourth, two chapters will address important features of the Christian life that follow from the obligations of membership of the church. Those chapters will address the importance of the preservation of the Sabbath day as a principal reason for the being of the church, and, as an example of ethical objectives of life within the church, the question of the swearing of oaths.

The following two chapters, titled "Does God Exist?" and "The Knowledge of God," take up and expand by way of illustration certain of the aspects of apologetic theology that have been anticipated in this chapter. It will be found, firstly, that the question whether God exists is not a proper question. That is because, in the first place, it is not a proper question on the grounds of its logical status. That is because, as was argued in the foregoing, the several proofs that it incorporates can be shown to be, in themselves, invalid. But secondly, the question whether God exists is a question that does not need to be asked. That is because, as the presuppositional scheme of apologetics acknowledges, God exists and has revealed himself, and the presupposition that *God is* is the starting point of all rational inquiry.

The principal conclusion of the next chapter is that it is possible only for the regenerate person to know God for who he is and how he has revealed himself. For the natural unregenerate man it is possible to know *that* God is, but not *who* God is.[12] That conclusion is thoroughly confirmed and illustrated in the opening chapter of Paul's letter to the Romans. The potential knowledge status that the individual person can acquire or command is determined by the fact that he is, as will be argued, the analogue of God as to both his being and his knowledge. His attainable knowledge, therefore, is

---

12. Christ himself made the point in his statement at Luke 10:22 that "No man knoweth . . . who the Father is, but the Son, and he to whom the Son will reveal him."

analogical of the knowledge that God possesses in himself. The knowledge capacities of man being given, and the distinctions between the regenerate and the unregenerate man being kept in view, the chapter will address also the question of how the good news of the gospel is to be presented. At that point, comment will be made on "the free offer of the gospel" in the light, as has been said, of the knowledge competence of the people to whom the gospel is presented.

Chapter 4 takes us in some detail to the heart of what we have indicated as the principal theologico-doctrinal question and problem we have in view. That, to recall only briefly, has to do with the significance of the human nature of Christ, his suffering on the cross in the *soulish aspect* of his human nature, and the relation of that to the total redemptive offering that Christ effected. Of prominent interest in those respects will be seen to be the participation in the redemption of the church of the triune Persons of the Godhead.

Following the arguments presented regarding the redemption of the church, two chapters address specific aspects of the system of doctrine confessed by the church. That is followed by some suggestions regarding the implied ethic and practice of the church or the members of it. The intention at those stages is to comment in different ways on the relation between what we have referred to as the church's evangel, on the one hand, and the evangelism or the actual presentation to the world of that system of doctrine or evangel on the other.

First, chapter 5 presents an expanded discussion of an issue that had been present, but substantially submerged, in preceding chapters. That has to do with the highly important respects in which the entire redemptive work of Christ in this world has covenantal significance. It will be shown that it was in accordance with the terms of a divine council of redemption before the foundation of the world that the Second Person of the Godhead came into the world to discharge the redemptive assignment to which he had voluntarily committed himself. What is referred to there as the covenant of redemption made it necessary that in order to accomplish its objectives, what we shall refer to as an implementing covenant should be brought to effect. That, as will be seen, was a covenant of grace, the parties to which were God on the one hand, and, on the other, the people he had ordained to be saved as represented by Christ. The discussion of the covenant that God has made with man is expanded in chapter 6 to the significance it holds for the on-going Christian life.

Chapter 7 turns to a fairly extended discussion of what must be regarded as a principal identifying aspect of the Christian church. That is the divine obligation laid on the church, as it can be shown to have been the repeated mandate of God throughout the entire Old Testament dispensation, that one day in seven should be reserved for the worship of God and for works pointed directly to that end. It need only be said at this stage that if the church should fail in its recognition of what is laid upon it in the fourth commandment of the Decalogue ("Remember the sabbath day to keep it holy") it has lost a profoundly important part of its primary defining characteristic. As the fourth commandment goes, so goes the integrity of the church.

One final point can be made at this stage in that respect. It will be argued that the Decalogue, the Ten Commandments as they were given by God to Moses, are to be seen as a republication and a rearticulation of the law of God as it had been given to our first parents in the garden. That being so, it is to be seen that the moral law, as it is encapsulated in the Ten Commandments, is to be understood as a *creation ordinance*. As a creation ordinance, and as it was given to man for his instruction and guidance, it remains obligatory on all people everywhere at all time.

Chapter 8 is presented as an example of the manner in which the body of truth we have examined to that point gives rise to certain ethical necessities. The example taken is that of the swearing of oaths, and the significance, meaning, and propriety of them.

A brief chapter on Conclusions will complete the book. In all, the following chapters, taken as a whole, aim to bring to increasingly meaningful focus what we have stated at the beginning as the relation between the evangel on the one hand and the church's evangelism, with the recognition of its responsibilities as the custodian of the evangel on the other.

Chapter 2

Does God Exist?

THE OBJECTIVE OF THE argument in this chapter is twofold: First, to consider whether the question in the title is itself a proper question. The answer on that level will be in the negative; and second, to raise certain issues that the question has for theological apologetics and for the Christian evangel and the church's evangelism. But to begin, several observations would seem to be necessary if anything meaningful is to be said in response to the question. First, it may seem odd that the question is posed at all in the context of Christian confession. Second, if, as has already been indicated, it may be concluded that the question itself is not a proper or meaningful question, what ground exists for that outcome? With that possible conclusion in view, however, it may be asked in the first instance whether the question posed is itself a *logically* proper or meaningful question. And then it may be asked, is there any ground at all, perhaps some such grounds as religion rather than logic, on which, or in relation to which, significance attaches to the question? Philosophers have argued the case. And theologians have frequently elided the issue, or with substantial lack of curiosity they have assumed and proceeded on the basis of a positive answer. If we take it that man is a rational, inquisitive, cognitive, ratiocinative being, surely the fact that our question can be and has been frequently raised requires us to take some serious notice of it.

The argument that follows will therefore look, first, at a theological answer to the question or an assumption regarding it; second, it will take account at a minimum level of certain traditional logical statements in response to the question; third, a return to the theological level will address what is to be held as the real status of the question; and fourth, a number of considerations will be noted that bear forcibly on the significance of the question for the church's evangelism.

A preliminary theological answer

Take, first, the relevance of theology proper, or, that is, what theologians refer to as the doctrine of God. That can be shown to take up many issues whose full elaboration lies beyond our present interest, but we shall return to some important implications of what is now said by way of summary. A late-seventeenth-century Puritan theologian, John Howe, states the point by way of definition: "We have the conception in our minds of *an eternal, uncaused, independent, necessary Being, that hath active power, life, wisdom, goodness, and whatever other supposable excellency, in the highest perfection originally, in and of itself.*"[1] The relevance of our question at this point is that the theological answer states that God exists as an *uncaused* being. That is what is involved in Howe's statement that God is a *necessary* being. Necessity, on the level now in view, means that God's existence is without cause. It is not being said that God is his own cause, or that he caused himself. If such an impossibility were held, it would then have to be said that God existed in order to have been, in turn, the cause of himself, or of his own existence.[2] We shall return to the point and reflect on the extent to which the answer to our initial question turns on the being, the revealed deliberations, and the decretive purposes of God.

When it is said that God is an *independent* being, or that he exists *independently*, it is being said that there does not exist any entity, law, or relation external to the Godhead to which God was subject, or which circumscribed his actions, in the determination of his will and his declared purpose. In the formation of the dictates of his will God did not, that is to say, choose between alternative possibilities to which he was then subsequently constrained in his further actions. There did not exist any "possibility" external to the Godhead. God created possibility. Only that became possible in human experience which God has declared, though, of course, human conception does not and cannot know *a priori* what God's sovereign will has declared and will in due course bring to pass.

What we have just said controverts the essential proposition of the "Open Theism" theology. That system of thought states that God is, in fact,

---

1. Howe, *Works*, I:27, italics original.
2. See ibid., 29.

ignorant of the future that will emerge from contingent human action. God is omniscient, the Open Theism agrees, but omniscience means, in that scheme of things, that God knows all that is available to be known. But as the future has not yet happened, it is not available to be known and God, therefore, does not, and cannot, know it. We argue, to the contrary, as Van Til has put it, that God thought all things in one eternal moment before the foundation of the world. It is not possible for man to do anything that God has not already thought. And further, it is not possible for man to *think* anything that God has not already thought.[3] God, that is, spoke into existence all that exists external to the Godhead, together with the laws of operation of that reality, including the laws of thought. What unfolds, therefore, in what is apparently human contingency, moves on the linear trajectory of divine intent.

Answers from philosophy

But let us turn to the question of the efficiency in relation to our question of the so-called logical or philosophic proofs that were referred to in the preceding chapter. In doing so, completeness of exposition is not intended, nor is a full elaboration of the logical niceties attaching to them. But a minimal indication of the explanatory competence, if any, they might be thought to provide is relevant to principal questions in hand.

Take, first, the *ontological proof of the existence of God*. That was first introduced by Anselm who flourished as the Archbishop of Canterbury in the late-eleventh century, and it was further developed by Descartes who is often referred to as the beginner of modern philosophy in the seventeenth century. The argument states, first, that it is possible to conceive of an entity, greater than which no other entity can be contemplated. That entity, it is then postulated, must be infinitely perfect, and perfection must necessarily involve its existence. The fallacy in the argument, as it has been widely recognized in the history of thought, is that "existence" cannot be said to be necessarily an attribute of perfection in what is conceived. As Berkhof has put it, "We cannot conclude from abstract thought to real existence."[4] What we see as the fallacy of the ontological proof bears resemblance to the well-known "Lessing's ditch," or the argument of the philosopher Gotthold Lessing in the mid- to late-eighteenth century that "the contingent truths of

---

3. Ezekiel 11:5, "I know the things that come into your mind, every one of them."
4. Berkhof, *Systematic Theology*, 26.

history can never become the proof of the necessary truths of reason."[5] But what we are advancing as the basis of reasoning for the regenerate mind, as that exists in submission to the revelation of God, not only carries us across Lessing's ditch, but in relation to the biblical truths that Lessing set out to destroy it eliminates it.

Second, a *cosmological proof of the existence of God* begins by recognizing that all entities that exist in the world are contingent, in the sense that they may quite well not have eventuated. To explain their existence, and omitting any possibility of self-causation, a preceding causal entity or entities must be posited. Readily recognizable, then, is the regress to an initial cause, which is then stated to be "God." I put the word "God" in quotation marks for reasons we shall see in a moment. The fallacy in the cosmological proof (as the late-Enlightenment philosopher, Kant, stated it), is that the cosmological proof depends on the prior assumption of the validity of the ontological proof we have just considered.[6] Before returning briefly to the point below, it can be observed that in any case the intellectual move to a first cause cannot be to any original entity greater than that capable of producing the effect considered. No adequate ground exists, therefore, to conclude that the initial cause contemplated can be designated the eternal God who has spoken into existence all things external to the Godhead.

The cosmological proof, then, or the argument to a first cause, fails for a twofold reason. First, it collapses at the point at which it implicitly leans on the ontological postulate; and second, while it may in the minds of its advocates reach the psychologically acceptable conclusion of an ultimate cause that is then designated "god," it has said something only about *a* "god," and nothing about the only true God who has revealed himself.

Third, a so-called *teleological proof of the existence of God*, or, as it is sometimes referred to, the *proof from design*, argues that what is observable in the world exhibits undeniable evidences of intelligence, harmony, and design, and therefore of purpose. That is assumed to argue, in turn, for the existence of a perfect designer. That designer, or architect, is then denominated "God." The fallacy in the proof exists, however, in the fact that even if the argument from the design to a designer were sustainable, it would establish only a very great designer, adequate to the necessities in view, and not necessarily an infinite or eternal or perfect designer of independent,

---

5. Cited in Krentz, *Historical-Critical Method*, 17.

6. Discussions abound in the relevant literature of the cogency of Kant's argument. See, for example, Smart, "The Existence of God."

necessary existence. If the latter step were to be made, it would depend again, as can readily be seen, on the prior conclusion of the so-called ontological proof.

It is not necessary to adduce at length other so-called proofs of God's existence. The moral proof that is mixed with an element of teleology, which contemplates a judgment and a righting in a world to come of this world's inequities and moral turpitudes, posits a law-giver and a judge. But that again founders on its concealed dependence on the ontological assumption.

While all that is so, the question has frequently been raised in evangelical circles whether those several theistic proofs do not have some evidential value. The answer needs to be carefully stated. After all, does not the Psalmist aver that "The heavens declare the glory of God, and the firmament showeth his handywork . . . There is no speech nor language where their voice is not heard" (Ps 19:1, 3). And did not the apostle Paul, the aristocrat of intellect, say that "The invisible things of him from the creation of the world are clearly seen, being understood by the things that are made, even his eternal power and Godhead" (Rom 1:20)? The argument itself could be expanded. But two things are to be said in response. First, the competence of such inductive-evidential arguments falls within the range of God's general revelation and self-testimony, and it rises to the level of assured truth only when the natural tendency to suppress that truth is eradicated from the human consciousness by the regenerating grace of God. Second, then, the proofs that we have briefly acknowledged can be said to provide what may be called "confirmatory evidence," meaning by that that they do confirm *in the regenerate mind* what has already been concluded on the grounds of God's revelation of himself and his purposes.

If any contrary conclusion were proposed, anything other than the fundamental apologetic presupposition that *God is* and that *he has spoken*, the underlying argument would be vitiated by the weight of its own methodology. That is because it can be shown to rest on the alternative apologetic presupposition of the explanatory competence of human reason. In other words, all such contrary arguments proceed implicitly from man to God, not, as Reformed theology in its finest expression holds, from God to man. Arguments of the former kind are essentially characterized by a theological rationalism. Berkhof, again, has stated as his principal theological presupposition at the beginning of his theistic argument that "For us the existence of God is the great presupposition of theology."[7]

Putting the "proofs" together, the absurdity they project, absurdity, that is, on the level of logic on which they proceed, lies in the fact that there is no necessary validity in the leap, as the ontological proof exhibits it, from observable reality to the existence of an infinite or perfect being. As has been said, existence cannot be assumed to be a necessary attribute of contemplatable entities. All that the classical theological "proofs" can achieve at their best is the notion of the existence of *a* god, not bearing any necessary resemblance to the true God who has given us a revelation of himself and his salvific purposes.

In view of what has been said to this point, it would seem, as was contemplated at the beginning, that the question we have posed—Does God exist?—is not a proper or meaningful question. The impropriety of the question resides in the fact that on the grounds of logic there is no possible answer to it. It seems that after all, we are locked in the conclusion that Kant reached in his so-called "Copernican revolution" in epistemology, or in the theory of knowledge and knowing, at the end of the eighteenth-century Enlightenment. To put that all too briefly, Kant confined the possibility of knowledge to what was perceivable in the "phenomenal realm," as he called it, the realm of things that could be seen and touched and handled; or more particularly and precisely, he confined knowledge to the *perception* of those things, as that perception was, in turn, advanced into knowledge by the interpretative application to it of certain so-called categories of mind, or categories of understanding that were present in the individual mind. It is crucial, in that scheme of things, to understand that what was in that way observed was the *perception* of things, or things as they appear to an observer, not the things in themselves. The things in themselves, the *ding an sich*, which lie beneath the sense-impressions that one receives, existed in what Kant referred to as the "noumenal realm." What existed in that realm was not an object of knowledge. In that realm, moreover, certain imaginable things which, in conception, were consigned to it may or may not exist. As to his theology proper, Kant consigned God to the noumenal realm and he concluded that God, therefore, may or may not exist. Because Kant's God was securely in the noumenal realm he was not an object of knowledge. He could not be known. Kant charitably concluded that while the existence of God could not be "proved," neither could it be disproved. In

---

7. Berkhof, *Systematic Theology*, 20.

his fuller philosophic theory, which does not detain us at this time, "God" was, for Kant, not a conclusion of pure reason, but a postulate or an assumption of practical reason.[8]

Religion versus reason

What, then, is to be said of the status of the question we have asked, Does God exist? If, as seems to be the case, no answer exists on the level of logic, or, that is, on the level of ordinary human epistemic inquiry, can importance and relevance be accorded the question on any other level? Some thinkers, for example Smart, in the paper referred to in a previous footnote, have argued that while the preceding "proofs" of logic are fallacious and incompetent, it is nevertheless true that in the case of "those who have the seeds of a genuinely religious attitude already within them . . . the argument from design . . . is a potent instrument in heightening religious emotion."[9] What is being said there is that while there does not exist any competent explanatory proof of the existence of God, a sense of religion conceivably conjures a proof, emotionally adequate to provide significance to life and thought and thereby to conduct and behavior. The situation thereby reached is clearly akin to that of Kant who, as has been seen, concluded that while the existence of God cannot be shown to be a conclusion of *pure reason*, it may be, and in Kant's larger argument it was, a useful if not necessary postulate of *practical reason.*

Or again, shifting the entire discussion and argument from the level of logic to that of religion brings into prominence shades of Schleiermacher's theology. In his *The Christian Faith*, for example, Schleiermacher's scheme of theology was structured around the concept of the individual's "feeling of absolute dependence" on God.[10] It may be relevant to observe that the motivation for Schleiermacher's work appears to have been the need to escape from the intellectualism with which Kant, in the immediately preceding years that came at the close of the eighteenth-century Enlightenment, had structured philosophic thought. But while Schleiermacher thereby rebelled

---

8. See a fuller discussion and literature references in Vickers, *Divine Purchase*, 17–18. Further comments on Kant's doctrine of God are contained in the following chapter in the context of references to Kant's *Critique of Pure Reason,* and *Critique of Practical Reason.*

9. Smart, "The Existence of God," 45.

10. Schleiermacher, *Christian Faith*, 12.

against the assumed autonomy of Kant's epistemology and his intellectualism, he replaced that with another autonomy based on the sovereignty of individual feeling, emotion, and subjectivity. The trap of subjectivity has vitiated forms of modern theology in the last century and a half.

It may be observed, as an addendum to what has been said of the philosophic interest in our subject, that an interesting philosophico-theological position has been taken by the development that occurred in the twentieth century. Paul Tillich, for example, in his *Systematic Theology*, addresses the question of the existence of God and concludes as follows: "The question of the existence of God can be neither asked nor answered. If asked, it is a question about that which by its very nature is above existence, and therefore the answer—whether negative or affirmative—implicitly denies the nature of God. It is as atheistic to affirm the existence of God as it is to deny it. God is being-itself, not *a* being."[11] We have commented in previous contexts on such related questions as the aseity, eternality, necessity, and independence of God. But it is beyond our present scope to survey extensively the literature of contemporary theology relevant to our present subject, or to note in detail the important anticipations of what has come down to us as the Reformed perspective.[12]

A theological-doctrinal conclusion

What, then, is to be said of our question? Our conclusion to this point is twofold. First, an unarguable proof of the existence of God can be stated and lies at the heart of a properly understood Christian theological apologetic. Second, however, it is an essential part of that proof that there is a profoundly important respect in which the question is still, in itself, improper. That, we shall see, resides in the fact that *the question never needs to be asked, because every person knows that God is*. Let us attempt to unravel briefly those two conclusions.

First, it is now proposed that an undeniable proof of the existence of God lies in what Christian apologists have referred to as the *impossibility of the contrary*. That argument as just stated is, as is well-known, an essential

---

11. Tillich, *Systematic Theology*, 237.

12. Helm, positing the existence of God, has produced an important monograph, *Eternal God*. See also Craig, *Time and Eternity*; Charnock, *Existence and Attributes*. For an extended discussion of the simplicity of God see Dolezal, *God without Parts: Divine Simplicity*, and *All that is in God*.

part of the presuppositional apologetic of the late Cornelius Van Til.[13] It is of interest in our present context that Van Til sets his argument against the so-called theistic proofs we have considered: "The true theistic proofs undertake to show that the idea of existence (ontological proof), of cause (cosmological proof), and purpose (teleological proof) are meaningless unless they *presuppose* the existence of God."[14] And in his *Common Grace*, Van Til fleshes out the same proposition: "To be constructed rightly, theistic proofs ought to presuppose the ontological trinity and contend that, unless we may make this presupposition, all human predication is meaningless. The words 'cause,' 'purpose,' and 'being,' used as universals in the phenomenal world, could not be so used with meaning unless we may presuppose the self-contained God."[15]

The impossibility of the contrary, therefore, turns on the postulate that unless the existence of God is presupposed, no possibility of predication of meaning exists. Such a conclusion turns on the truth of the *imago Dei* in man and the consequent nature of his epistemic capacity and potential. We shall explore that further in a moment. That knowledge potential is to be understood as it existed, first, in man's paradisaic, prelapsarian state, then as he was fallen, and then subsequently as regenerate and redeemed. But let us put in a further way the proof of the impossibility of the contrary.

Consider for a moment the contrary assumption, the assumption that God does not exist and has not therefore ordained and ordered all that comes to pass (Eph 1:11). Then it must be asked: If God does not exist, what contrary explanation of existent reality and the history of reality is possible? The answer can only be that in such a case all that eventuates is the result of chance, and that it comes into being as a result of inexplicable processes of chance. Chance is then king and random processes are his servants. All eventuation is chance phenomena. But if chance is king, there is no reason why what is, or what has been, might not have existed and occurred at all. It could have been entirely different. But more significantly, if all entities and existences are the product of chance, then man himself is a chance phenomenon. That, then, implies the destruction of human personhood and the destruction of human responsibility and accountability. It implies the destruction of ethics. It would be a short step to explain that in such a

---

13. See Van Til, *Defense of the Faith*; Bahnsen, *Van Til's Apologetic*.

14. Van Til, *Common Grace*, 190. Cited in Bahnsen, *Van Til's Apologetic*, 621, italics added.

15. Van Til, *Common Grace*, 49.

direction lies the essential results of what has become referred to in recent times as postmodernism. Postmodernism, it can be readily shown, has proceeded beyond the theological fad of half a century ago that argued for the "death of God" to what is now effectively the death of man. Man is dead in the postmodern scheme of things because, as a result of the dominating explanatory significance of chance, there does not exist, it is claimed, any continuous human nature or identity. The result of such an analysis, if the essential indeterminism that characterizes postmodernism can be called analytic, is that modern thought has confused the reality that while there is an *epistemic discontinuity* in the human self, there is an *ontological continuity*.

But the question persists. What is now to be seen as the relevance of our argument to the conclusion of the being and existence of God? The argument from the impossibility of the contrary is confirmed by a twofold reality that comes to focus on the levels we have adduced. First, God is, because God has revealed himself. It is not necessary at this point to trace out the facts that, and the ways in which, God has made a self-revelation to man. He has revealed himself, not only in the universe of reality that he spoke into existence, where all of reality bears the imprint of the hands of God, not only in man himself whom he created as his own image, not only in the history of the human race that he has providentially ordered, but in the Scriptures that constitute his articulated word, and definitively, in the coming into the world and the salvific work of his Son. The eternal Second Person of the Godhead came into this world to become Jesus Christ for our redemption. The terms and processes of that revelation do not call for extensive rehearsal at this time.

But it is well known that Christian apologetics, even among those of Reformed theological persuasion, have presented contrary and, we are bound to say, erroneous conclusions on these issues. What has just been stated implies that the fundamental apologetic presupposition to be held is that *God is* and that *God has spoken*. It has to be said, on the other hand, that the fundamental apologetic presupposition of an evidentialist approach, that was referred to briefly in the preceding chapter, is that of the competence of human reason. Evidentialism as a system of thought argues from man to God instead of from God to man. It forgets that man by searching cannot find out God. God does not exist at the end of a logical syllogism or a chain of human inquiry. That way points to a theological rationalism. It is building a bridge without foundation at one end and reaching into nothing at the other end.

But that is not all that is to be said. We have said that there remains a significant sense in which our question, Does God exist? is not, finally, a proper question. That, as we now see it, is because *the question needs never to be asked*. Why is that conclusion, it may be asked, relevant in the argument we have adopted in what has been said to this point? The answer is more significantly important and conclusive than, there is reason to regret, our theology frequently acknowledges or takes into account. Let us explore the issue briefly. It has to do with the nature of man himself, the status in which he came from the hands of his Creator, and the manner of his being and conduct in the world.

In brief, every man knows that God is. When Adam came to self-consciousness he knew, with a necessary reflex of awareness, that he was the creature of a Creator God. Our first parent was established as the image of God, consciously aware that he imaged God in his being, aware that he was covenantally responsible to God, and capable of thinking God's thoughts after him. Adam was created as a covenant creature. For him, to *be* was to *know*. In his paradisaic, prelapsarian state he automatically knew God. Adam, as the image of God, thought and spoke because God thought and spoke. He was established in an inherent and essential state of holiness because God is holy. He was naturally aware of a sense of obligation and morality because God is moral.

Further, as to the faculties of soul in which he was established, with the intellectual faculty Adam naturally knew God, with the affective faculty he naturally loved God, and with the volitional faculty he naturally obeyed God. There existed a natural harmony among the faculties of the soul. The mind was the prince of the faculties. That is to say, as "God walked with Adam in the garden in the cool of the day" (Gen 3:8) in the Person of the Second Person of the Godhead in preincarnate form, he communed with Adam and explained to him what was required of him that he might discharge to the glory of God the offices of prophet, priest, and king in which he had been established. Adam was to be a prophet under God in that he was to investigate and explain the meaning of the reality in which he had come to self-awareness; he was to discharge the office of priest in that, having direct access to God, he was to dedicate back to the glory of God the explanation of reality that he discovered; and he was to live as a king under God in that he was to reign with dominion over all that God has created.

But our first parent fell into sin. The report of the event is familiar. "Of man's first disobedience, and the fruit of that forbidden tree whose mortal taste brought death into the world, and all our woe . . ." is how John Milton records it in his immortal *Paradise Lost*.[16] As a result of that primeval fall, the harmony of the faculties of the soul was shattered and the hegemony of the mind was replaced by that of the lusts and passions of the soul. Such was the sorry state to which we were reduced by Adam's fall. That sorry state inheres in the twofold results that followed. First, the guilt of Adam's first sin (not his subsequent sins) was imputed to, placed to the account of, all of his natural posterity. And second, the fallen nature in which Adam now existed was transmitted to all of that posterity.[17]

The human status and the point of contact

But what, we must now ask, is the relevance to our initial question of the conclusion that man as he now exists is the beneficiary of the effects of Adam's fall and that he lives, therefore, in a state of sin? Our answer to that question has profound implications, not only for our theological apologetic or our defense of the faith, but for our entire program and process of evangelism. Let us comment on the apologetic question first.

Let it be granted, as is clearly the case by biblical diagnosis, that by reason of the fall into sin, man is disabled in all of the faculties of the soul. The mind, the intellectual faculty, is "blinded by the god of this world" (2 Cor 4:4); as to the affective faculty, "the heart of man is deceitful above all and desperately wicked" (Jer 17:9); and the will, the volitional faculty, is subject to the bondage of Satan and sin—"Ye are of your father the devil, and the lusts of your father ye will do" (John 8:44); "Whoever commits sin is the slave of sin" (John 6:34). Man in his natural state is altogether turned away from God. "There is no fear of God before their eyes" (Rom 3:18). The case could be examined at length. "The natural man receiveth not the things of the Spirit of God; for they are foolishness unto him; neither can he know them, because they are spiritually discerned" (1 Cor 2:14).

The question that follows (and that question is being put for a moment on the level of theological apologetics) is that if that biblical diagnosis of unregenerate man in his natural state is correct, how, then, is it possible for

---

16. Milton, *Paradise Lost*, lines 1–3.

17. The *Westminster Shorter Catechism*, Question 16, was stated in Chapter 1 to that effect.

any statement of the gospel or of God's revelation to make any contact with him? That is at rock bottom the apologetic question, and the answer needs to be clearly stated. Let us state the question as bluntly as possible. Is there any point of contact, and if so, what is the point of contact between the believer and the unbeliever, between man as he stands in sin and condemnation under God and the good news of the gospel?

We have said that man as he came from the hands of his Creator was the image of God. Clearly, certain aspects of that image were lost in the fall, man's original, inherent, and essential righteousness and his natural knowledge of God. But the image as such remains and persists. Man is still a rational, immortal, spiritual, moral, and speaking person who in those respects images his Creator to whom he remains responsible. God, moreover, has kept open the channels of communication to man as his image, and the reality that is involved in that gives us the answer to our question.

The human status, the fact that man as he came from the hands of his Creator was the image of God, and that notwithstanding the fall that status of image remains in the sense we have stated, can be summed up in a further descriptive statement of human personhood. We have it, in 2 Corinthians 4:4 for example, that *Christ* is the image of God. Does propriety exist, then, in stating that *man* is the image of God? We have already answered in the affirmative. Jesus Christ is clearly, on the copious revelation of the pages of Scripture, the *infinite and essential* image of God, meaning by *essential* that the full essence of the Godhead resides in him. But man, on the other hand, is the *finite and derivative* image of God. Man is the derivative analogue of God as to both his being and his knowledge. We shall return to a correlative implication of human personhood when account is taken of the Holy Spirit's work on and within the faculties of the soul in the conveyance of the grace of regeneration. Human personhood exists in that man is in possession of, and capable of, reflective self-awareness, purposive action, and the consciousness of moral responsibility.

But what, we are now asking, is the *point of contact* between man in his fallen state on the one hand and God, or between the unbeliever and what the gospel has to say to man? The point of contact is not the fact of the image of God, the *imago Dei*, as such. It is something that resides within the image, that is inherent in the very created constitution of man from which it is impossible for him to escape. The point of contact is the sense of God, the *sensus deitatis*, that is embedded in the soulish consciousness of every man. In short, every man knows, with an indelible awareness that cannot be voluntarily erased, that *God is*. Moreover, every man knows that he is under obligation to God, that he has not fulfilled those obligations, and that he is accountable to God for not having done so. The first chapter of Paul's letter to the Romans is eloquent on the point and bears close investigation. There are no atheists. The statement can be expanded to observe that what is intended is that there are no *psychological* atheists, meaning again that every man knows in the depths of his soul that *God is*. Of course, there are what we might refer to as practical atheists, people who live as though there is no God. That specific case is undoubtedly all too widespread. But as Van Til has expressively stated it, "The most depraved of men cannot wholly escape the voice of God. . . The prodigal son can never forget the father's voice. It is the albatross forever about his neck."[18]

In stating those conclusions, it is not being said that every man is always and everywhere conscious of the being and presence of God. Of course not. We have already acknowledged as much in the reference to practical atheism. But what is being said is that the moral consciousness of every man is subject to agitation via his embedded conscience that is the moral monitor of the soul, though the sensibilities of conscience have themselves been damaged by the defects of sin. But when, from time to time, the *sensus deitatis* is awakened, and the awareness of God rises unbidden to the level of consciousness, what, we ask on the level of scriptural data, is man's natural reaction? The answer is that man naturally suppresses, pushes down, smothers, and does anything he can to suppress that awareness. He naturally loves darkness rather than light. He naturally wants nothing to do with God. The apostle to the Romans has explained the case: "The wrath of God is revealed from heaven against all ungodliness and unrighteousness of men, who by their unrighteousness *suppress the truth*" (Rom 1:18, ESV).

It follows from what has been said that the recognition of the existence of God that arises from the imperative of the *sensus deitatis* is not simply a warrantless assertion. It is an inevitable response of soulish consciousness that accords with the inherent character of created human being and identity. Beyond what is to be regarded, in the manner stated, as the conviction of divine being that accrues to everyman, for the person to whom God by his Spirit has conveyed the grace of regeneration an entirely new dimension of meaning and cognition opens. The Scriptures state the case copiously. The Psalmist anticipated fuller revelation when he said that "In thy light shall we see light" (Ps 36:9). The regenerate mind commands certainties of

---

18. Van Til, "Nature and Scripture, 266–67.

apprehension, illumination of divine verities, that the unregenerate mind knows, and can know, nothing about (1 Cor 2:14, 16).[19] Now, by reason of that regenerating grace, new dimensions of what we have recognized as reflective self-awareness, new levels of consciousness of moral obligation, and new parameters of purposive action and the holy ends which that contemplates, inform the human character.

Evangelism

The terms of the gospel are clear and clearly articulated in the word that God has given. But the questions remain: How is that gospel to be stated in the hearing of sinners who stand so urgently in need of reconciliation with God and in need of the redemption that God has provided in his Son? And how, in that urgency, do the conclusions we have reached as to the being and existence of God bear on the presentation of the gospel?

The gospel, whose terms are spread liberally across the pages of Scripture, does not call for extensive rehearsal in our present context. But a number of things that bear immediately on what has been argued to this point can be said. First, while the gospel is addressed to man, the first statement of the gospel is not a statement about man. The gospel is addressed to man in sin, but the first statement of the gospel is not a statement about sin. The gospel presents the redeeming work of Christ as the way of reconciliation with God and salvation from sin, but the first statement of the gospel is not a statement about Jesus Christ and his work in this world. Let us look at the way in which the apostle John has stated the case.

John, he says at the beginning of his first epistle, was among those who had traveled with Christ from the beginning, who had seen and touched him in his incarnate identity, had heard the words of life he had come to declare, and had learned from him. Now John sets out to pass on the message of life to those to whom he wrote. "This then is the message," he begins, and he is clearly careful and particular in his order of statement. "This then is the message which we have heard of him, and declare unto you, that God is light, and in him is no darkness at all" (1 John 1:5). God, John is saying as the first statement of what he had to report, is a holy God. It is a holy God with whom man has to do, a God living in light that no man can approach, that cannot bear in any unmediated manner on the eyes or the souls of

---

19. See an extended Argument in Vickers, *Discovering the Christian Mind*, 1–103.

men. The first statement of the gospel, then, as John teaches us to state it, is a statement about God.

In similar terms, the first statement of the gospel is a statement about the creative activity of God who spoke into existence all things external to the Godhead. It is a statement, therefore, that all that God creatively established, all men and things, are God's property. All men, therefore, are under obligation to God and sustain an accountability to God.

Those preliminary data bear with immediate relevance on the question we have addressed. Does God exist? we have asked. Yes, God exists, we answer. And our answer turns on the grounds of God's own self-revelation and on the clear revelation that he has made, on his own declaration regarding the *sensus deitatis* indelibly embedded in the soul of everyman. By the sovereign awakening of the Holy Spirit in his ministry to the soul, the awareness of God is raised to the level of human consciousness. When the Holy Spirit accompanies that wakening awareness by conveying to the sinner the grace of regeneration, a new life has come into being, and the sinner now sees and understands what before had no meaning to him. He sees that he stands nakedly exposed in soul before a holy God. He now knows the meaning of his sin and his undoneness, his lost estate. By the secret, sovereign, and unsolicited regenerating grace of the Spirit of God he is now a new creature (2 Cor 5:17). He finds that now, with newness of mind that was before dead to the grace of God, he wants to reach for newness of life with God; he now knows God in a manner that before was in no sense possible. He now finds his whole intellectual and emotional complex reaching out to express love for God at the same time as he hates his sin. He now has only one new motivation. He wants to know the new life that comes with the "living water" that Christ provides (John 4:11). He now wants only Christ.

But what, further, does the gospel state to man, to unregenerate man in his natural state of sin? Confining our comments to the context of our initial questions, two things are to be said. First, as we have stated it, there is a residual sense in which the question, Does God exist? does not need to be asked. The reason for that, we have said, is that every man knows that God exists, and we have attempted to lay out the justification for that conclusion. Second, it follows that because the *sensus deitatis* in man bears testimony to the existence of God, if, when the gospel of God's grace is presented to him he rejects it and attempts to controvert and suppress the awakening conviction it brings, he is living a lie. That is the rock-bottom implication that must be made clear. The man who rejects the convicting awareness and demands of God is engaged in living a lie. By his suppression of the truth that he constitutionally knows, by his claim that the truth itself is a lie, he is not only fooling himself but is laying the foundation for greater condemnation against himself in the day of final reckoning and accountability.

A concluding implication

Let us ask, in conclusion, What is the result for life in the everyday that the knowledge of God provides? To do that we refer to an old Greek philosopher and mathematician named Archimedes. Archimedes flourished in the third century before Christ and in the history of thought he is famous for, among other things, his discovery of the principle of the lever. With the consciousness of that principle in view he is renowned for having stated: "Give me a place on which to stand and I will move the world." Now if it were possible to satisfy Archimedes' request, the point on which he should stand would have to be extramundane. He could not move the world by standing on a point within the world. The point on which to stand must be outside the world. We are accordingly interested in what has become referred to in the history of thought as the Archimedean point.

The concept of the Archimedean point has particular application to the inquiry in which we have been engaged. We are interested now in what can be called the Christian's Archimedean point. By that we mean a point on which the Christian can stand in his thought system in order, not to *move* the world in the original Archimedean sense, but to *understand* the world and thereby understand himself. Again, in a sense similar to what we have said, such a point must be, for the Christian, an extramundane point. That is clearly true in the sense that the Christian has come to realize above all else that the thought systems of the world do not, and they cannot, provide a basis for understanding life and reality. That is why the apostle, in the opening chapters of his first letter to the Corinthians, has differentiated the wisdom of the world from the wisdom of God. "The Greeks seek after wisdom" (1 Cor 1:22). But Paul was interested, not in "words of man's wisdom" or "the wisdom of this world" (1 Cor 2:4, 6), but in "the hidden wisdom which God ordained before the world" (1 Cor 2:7). When Paul came to the Corinthians he was, as he said, "determined not to know anything among you save Jesus Christ and him crucified" (1 Cor 2:2). For as he stated to the Colossians, in Christ "are hid all the treasures of wisdom and knowledge" (Col 2:3).

That being said, what, we now ask, is understandable as the Christian's Archimedean point, the place on which he can stand in order to understand the world? It cannot, again, be an intramundane point. It cannot be a point provided by any thought systems of the world. It must be, and must come from, outside the world. To answer our question, let us refer to our Lord's high priestly prayer that he prayed in the hearing of his disciples on the night on which he was betrayed. He said to the Father: "I have manifested thy name unto the men which thou gavest me out of the world. Thine they were, and thou gavest them me; *and they have kept thy word*" (John 17:6). In that statement we find the answer to our question. The Christian knows and "keeps" the word of God. That is his Archimedean point. It has come completely from outside the world. It has come from the only true God who spoke the world into existence. The Christian stands on the word of God, and doing so he understands what before was darkness and confusion to him and was only the way of death and despair. Now he sees and knows and has life eternal, for as our Lord again prayed in that memorable prayer: "This is life eternal, that they might know thee the only true God, and Jesus Christ whom thou hast sent" (John 17:3).

We have said that standing on his Archimedean point of the word of God, the Christian acquires levels of understanding that were previously entirely closed to him. Let us put that differently in closing. We have spoken at an earlier point of our first parent's first estate and his subsequent fall into sin. The meaning and implications of that fall can be characterized in many ways. But for our present purposes we can say that at the fall Adam lost the true principles and categories of understanding and meaning that he had enjoyed. He lost the criteria of truth and validity in knowledge. Now that the Spirit of God has come to a man in regenerating grace, and now that the Spirit has worked his effects in and on all the faculties of the soul, there are again many ways of characterizing the results and effects. But consistently with our present inquiry, one highly important effect can be stated. It is that the born-again individual (John 3:5) has restored to him the true principles and categories of meaning and interpretation that Adam lost at the fall. He now has access to the true criteria of truth and validity in knowledge. Now, knowing God revealed in his Son by the ministry to him of the Holy Spirit, the Christian sees and understands all things through the lens provided by his knowledge of God in Christ.

Does God Exist?

The question was asked at the beginning, Does God exist? We saw that the thought schemes of the world and the logic of philosophic inquiry were not competent to provide an answer. They only sidetracked the inquirer into a blind alley and an intellectual dead end. We saw also that not only for the Christian but for man in general, an important sense exists in which the question itself is without point. That is because the question does not need to be asked. And that, in turn, is because every man knows that God is, by reason that God has kept open the lines of communication to man, response to which turns on the ineradicable sense of God, the *sensus deitatis* embedded in the soul.

Chapter 3

The Knowledge of God

TWO QUESTIONS HAVE LONG engaged reflective minds. The questions of *being* (or what is the "real," or what is the object of metaphysical inquiry) and *knowing* (or the epistemological inquiry into the origin, processes, and validity of knowledge) have long occupied active minds. Perhaps it is fair to say that in modern times, particularly since the so-called "Copernican revolution" in the theory of knowledge proposed by Immanuel Kant in the late-eighteenth century, the latter has swamped out the former. What it comes to on the level of the present inquiry into the knowledge of God is, first, the question of the competence of the human mind to grasp a knowledge of who God is in his being and self-revelation, and second, that of what is to be said, if anything in that direction is possible, of God's actions and purposes in relation to the world of time. For it is clear that *time is*. If time is not eternal, then time must have itself come into being, or be a created entity. In that case, thought has posited a Creator.

Let it be posited (as will be submitted in due course as a necessary postulate) that *God is*, and that he is eternal. The question then becomes that of the status of human being in relation to the possibility of knowing God, of what is to be held as the origin of that possibility, and of what are the processes by which such knowledge is attainable and how its validity criteria are to be stated. In short, what we are concerned with is the relation between the possible *object* of knowledge, God and his purposes, and man as the *subject* of knowledge. Taking together God in his necessary eternal being and time as a created entity, we are asking: Is temporal knowledge of the eternal God possible, and what is to be understood as its potential scope and validity?

The Knowledge of God

To answer the question now before us, that of the relation between the *object* and the *subject* of knowledge as stated, between God and man, it is necessary to reflect on what is to be said regarding the being of God and the self-revelation he has made, and the being and origin of man as the creature of God. When the question is stated in those terms, it must be borne in mind that it is possible, however, to interpret the question of the knowledge of God in two ways. First, the statement with which we began may be conjured as a *subjective genitive*, meaning by that that the "of God" refers to the knowledge that God himself possesses. God, that is, is taken to be himself the *subject*, not the *object* of knowledge. If, on the contrary, the statement is understood to be stating an *objective genitive*, then man, not God, is the subject of knowledge, and God and his ways are the object of knowledge. In that case we are contemplating the possibility of man's knowledge of God. We shall see in what follows that both those possibilities of interpreting our question exist and are meaningful. For we shall be concerned with the relation between the knowledge that God himself possesses and the possibility of the human mind's coming into possession of that knowledge.

Aligning our thought now with that of historic theological inquiry, and reflecting, as the apostle to the Romans stated by clear implication (Romans 1) on the being of God, the opening postulate of a late-Puritan author whom we quoted previously provides our focus: "We have the conception in our minds of *an eternal, uncaused, independent, necessary Being, that hath active power, life, wisdom, goodness, and whatever other supposable excellency, in the highest of perfection originally, in and of itself.*"[1] We have commented that when we say that God is a "necessary Being" we are saying that he is uncaused, that in his independent existence he does not depend for his being on any thing or entity or principle or possibility external to himself. We are referring to the *aseity* of God, to the fact that he is *a se*, or of himself. As the seventeenth-century Westminster assembly stated it, "God is a spirit, infinite, eternal, and unchangeable, in his being, wisdom, power, holiness, justice, goodness, and truth."[2]

What is being said is that no point is to be served by setting out to "prove" the existence of God. The classical so-called theological proofs do not call for extended rehearsal, the ontological, cosmological, moral, or teleological "proofs." We have already taken note of them in a previous context. For our conclusion is that God has made a self-revelation

---

1. Howe, *Works*, 1:27, italics in original.
2. *Westminster Shorter Catechism*, Question 4.

and a revelation of his purposes and ordinations in various ways. He has done that in the created environment in which we live, in history, in the Scriptures that he has caused to be written (and of which he, in the Person of his Holy Spirit, is the primary author), in, as we shall see, the human consciousness, and, most notably, in the appearance in this world of his Son. The second Person of the Godhead came into this world to become Jesus Christ for the redemption of the people whom the Father gave to him before the foundation of the world (John 17:6, 9). The Scriptures, that is to say, do not set out to prove the existence of God. They present us with the statement that *God is*. "In the beginning God . . ." (Gen 1:1; see John 1:1). "*God is*" is our fundamental apologetic presupposition.

As to man, we posit that he is a creature made in the image of his Creator God. The catechism that we have already cited explains that "God created man, male and female, after his own image, in knowledge, righteousness, and holiness, with dominion over the creatures."[3] We shall observe that man is the image of God in that he is a rational, immortal, spiritual, moral, and speaking person. It is in that last-mentioned characteristic that the image of God most pointedly exists. For man thinks and speaks because God thinks and speaks. And it is in the act of speaking that God makes himself known. The endowment of speech permits man to hear and respond to the speech of God.

Man created and fallen

Following what has just been said, we can now ask what is to be concluded regarding man's capacity for knowing and, as we have stated it, his knowing God? The necessary answer turns on the understanding of man as he came from the hands of his Creator and, as it is necessary to contemplate, his status in the condition of sin into which he fell. It is necessary to bear in mind that man as created stands in covenantal relation with God. The concept of the covenant is our basic hermeneutical principle.[4] Man is a covenant creature, created in time that was in turn established as a mode of finite existence.

When it is said that God created man as his own image, it is necessary to hold that man stands in an analogical relation to God. That is to say, he is

---

3. Ibid., Question 10.

4. The concept of "covenant" and its doctrinal relevance is discussed more fully in chapter 5.

like God but he is not *identical* with God. He mirrors or images in himself certain characteristics which in themselves are Godlike. For instance, as has been said, man thinks and speaks because God thinks and speaks. He is capable of moral decisions and actions because God is moral. He is a spiritual being because God is spirit. In his primeval state, man was holy because God is holy. That is, man as created was intrinsically holy, constitutionally holy. His holiness was not, contrary to certain errant theological claims, a *donum superadditum*, a gift "added on" to him after he had been created. The importance of that statement is that the *donum superadditum* claim carries with it a defective understanding of the implication of our first parent's fall into sin. For if Adam's original holiness was simply something "added on" after he had been created, the meaning of the fall is that, by his sin, Adam lost that original endowment and, as a result, was reduced to the state in which he had been at first established before the gift of holiness was "added-on" to him. To make such a claim is to evade completely the meaning, not only of our first parent's sinful state, but also that of the ongoing capacities of soul that resulted. In particular, as we now have it, the differences of view we have contemplated are related to differences of understanding as to man's will, and in turn they imply differences of intellectual capacity that is relevant to man's potential knowledge.

Consider man's state of soul as he was originally created. When we have said that he is the image of God, a spiritual being capable of communication with God, we are required to contemplate both the *soulish aspect* and the *bodily aspect* of his standing, as they contributed to the explanation of his being or personhood. As to his soulish aspect, man possessed the faculties of intellect, emotion, and will. The soul is capable of thought, affection, and volition, or as is frequently said, the soul is mind, heart, and will. It is important at that point to acknowledge the necessary interrelations between the respective faculties, the intellectual, affective, and volitional. In human action, the intellectual and affective faculties are operative in recognizing possible courses of action, evaluating the pressures and desirability of each, and instructing the will to act. That conclusion was the essential outcome of Jonathan Edwards' treatise on the freedom of the will in the eighteenth century that established him as the foremost American philosopher-theologian of his time.[5] We leave aside Edwards' extensive development to observe that the will, as Edwards stated, is not capable of independent action. The will acts as it is instructed by the intellectual and emotional judgments

---

5. Edwards, *Freedom of the Will*, 1996.

that are made by an individual at any given point in time. The will acts, that is, consistently with what the intellect and the emotions advise to it as the most desirable or the putatively most beneficial course of action. Edwards observed that "it is impossible for the will to choose contrary to its own preponderating inclination,"[6] or, in other words, the will acts in accordance with what is contemplated to be its "greatest apparent good."[7] But for the decision-moment, and for the possible action at the point of the individual person's decision, the action contemplated is deemed by the person to be the most desirable. That "most desirable" action may in itself, of course, and considered on certain objective grounds, not be in the ultimate best interests of the person making the decision and choice (for example, excessive drinking). But nevertheless, the action as specified may appear to be, in the individual's mind and taking into account his emotional disposition at the time of decision, the most preferred choice. That Edwardsian argument in itself clarifies the essential intention of his work. For the principal objective he had in view in his treatise was to controvert the claims of a sub-biblical theological doctrine that was part of Arminianism. For it is the essential claim of that scheme of things that the will is capable of determining its own action, independently of the intellectual and affective faculties.

If, now, we ask what are to be understood as principal characteristics of the soul in its prelapsarian state, two observations are to be made. First, there existed a natural harmony of the faculties. With the intellectual faculty, our first parent naturally knew God, with the affections he naturally loved God and sought after what pleased God, and with the will he naturally obeyed God. Second, the intellect, or the mind, was the prince of the faculties of the soul. That last-mentioned conclusion brings us to the principal point now under discussion. That is the princedom, the hegemony, of the mind. That princedom is established and confirmed by the twofold facts: First, in exhibition of man's capacity for speech as an aspect of his identity as the image of God, God "walked with Adam in the garden in the cool of the day" (Gen 3:8), and in doing so he communicated to Adam what was required of him in order that he should be pleasing to God; and second, in such a naturally harmonious relation God conveyed to Adam not only what he should do as God's vicegerent in the preservation and development of the universe, but also the laws of morality. Those laws were to be

---

6. Ibid., 79.
7. Ibid., 86.

republished and rearticulated in the moral law, the Ten Commandments, as they were given to Moses in codified form.

But sin entered the world, and its entailment is copiously declared in the Scriptures. The action of our first parents that constituted the sin was, in its essence, a matter of intellection as it was a moral act. For when Adam was confronted with the temptation to eat of the forbidden fruit (Gen 2:16–17) there stood before him competing advices from God and Satan respectively. At that point, Adam decided that he would not accept, obey, or follow the advice of either, simply on the ground of the identity of the one offering the advice. Rather, he would decide his own course of action. He would, in other words, assert his autonomy. And that, in its essence, is the meaning of sin. Sin is the individual's assertion of autonomy against God. It is, in another aspect, the repudiation of covenantal obligations to God.

The state of soul in what is now its fallen capacity is such that the hegemony of the mind as previously observed has been replaced by the hegemony of the lusts and the passions. That is because, as to the level of intellect, "the god of this world hath blinded the minds of them which believe not" (2 Cor 4:4). Man is now the blinded dupe and the slave of Satan and sin. Our Lord stated it clearly to the Jews on one occasion: "Ye are of your father the devil, and the lusts of your father ye will do" (John 8:44). The upshot, as to man in his fallen state, is as the apostle, Paul, put it: "The natural man receiveth not the things of the Spirit of God; for they are foolishness unto him; neither can he know them because they are spiritually discerned" (1 Cor 2:14). Such is the sorry state of incapacity in which man stands as a result of the fall.

To know God

Against the propositions and conclusions we have stated to this point, we return to our original questions: First, is it possible for man to know God, and to know God as he is in himself; and second, is it possible for man to know what God knows? We take the first question first.

The foregoing implies that the question of man's knowledge of God cannot be answered without prior reference to the identity and status of the man that is involved. We have seen that in his prelapsarian state man naturally knew God. But it follows equally that in his postlapsarian or fallen state it is impossible for man to know God. That is the differentiating characteristic that calls for explanation. By the knowledge of God, we intend the knowledge of who God is in the attributes of identity and grace that he has revealed to man. In short, the natural man *does not* and, on the basis of the scriptural data we have adduced (1 Cor 2:14), he *cannot* know God. What is involved is important, not only on the level of apologetic theology, but in relation also to the church's announcement of the gospel of grace, of which it has been made the custodian.

The issue that arises can be put concisely by stating that an antithesis exists between the natural unregenerate man and the man who has been made regenerate by the revivifying and illuminating grace of God. It follows from the explanation of the bonded state of man in sin that, as the Corinthian text has already stated, it is simply impossible for the person who is the enslaved dupe of the devil to know the things of God, or to know, that is, what God has declared of himself and his purposes in his self-revelation. Of such a person, it is to be said, of course, that he is essentially religious. By reason of the consciousness and capacities of soul in which he was created, man naturally proposes to himself some one or the other god. That "god" may be material, an idol of wood or stone as was the case all too frequently in the history of God's people (Jer 3:8–9). Or the object of worship may be any of a number of immaterial objects, such as money, reputation, family, or socio-cultural identity and status.

By reason of his created identity, that is, every man will naturally hold to a true or a false religion, either a religion that is addressed to the true God, or an apostate religion. But deep in the human consciousness lies the conviction, in varying degrees, that the true God exists and has a covenantal claim on man, his creature. The difference in the respective cases in view turns, as has been anticipated, on the status of an individual as still existing in his natural unregenerate state or regenerate by the grace of God. In short, as will be concluded, the regenerate man knows God. The unregenerate man does not. It is not necessary to unfold at length at this point the meaning and operation of the regenerating grace of God as that works in the soul of the individual to establish the difference of personhood that we have in view. It will suffice to note the following.

First, the possibility and the fact of the regenerate person's knowledge of God has been clearly stated by our Lord himself. In his high priestly prayer in the presence of his disciples on the night on which he was betrayed he stated to the Father: "This is life eternal, that they might know thee the only true God, and Jesus Christ whom thou hast sent" (John 17:3). To know God is, in this world, man's highest good, his *summum bonum*.

In the eternal day to come, those whom God has drawn to himself will *see* God in the face of Jesus Christ. While at present God's people do not *see* him with the eyes of flesh, they nevertheless do *know* him.

Second, the manner in which the grace of regeneration stands behind the new identity of the Christian who now *knows* God, has been stated by the apostle to the Colossian church in the following form. "The Father . . . hath delivered us from the power of darkness, and hath translated us into the kingdom of his dear Son" (Col 1:13).

But the lack of clarification of the knowledge question as it stands has diminished at times the testimony of the church and the statement of the good news of the gospel. By that it is meant that there has been observable all too often in the announced doctrinal teaching of the church a tendency to offer that gospel to man on the assumption that no difference exists between the knowledge capacities of the unregenerate and the regenerate person. The offer of the gospel is frequently made on the assumption that it is possible for all men everywhere to know God and, in that context, to freely accept or reject the offered mercy of God, as he has set that forth in the salvific work of his Son. But such a procedure neglects entirely what we have observed as the antithesis between the regenerate and the unregenerate man. It assumes that there exists, on the human level, such a thing as reason-in-general, and therefore the possibility of the acquisition of knowledge, in which both the unregenerate and regenerate share. Nothing could be further from the truth.

As to the possibility of knowledge, and referring to the difference between the unregenerate and the regenerate person, the mid-twentieth-century apologetic theologian, Cornelius Van Til, as we noted in the brief discussion of apologetics in chapter 1, put the difference in a sentence: "Metaphysically, both parties have all things in common, while epistemologically they have nothing in common."[8] Who is it, then, who can know God? The answer is the person whom God has drawn to himself as our Lord has said: "No man can come unto me, except the Father which hath sent me draw him" (John 6:44); and the grace of God is displayed in the statement of Christ in the same context: "All that the Father giveth to me shall come to me; and him that cometh to me I will in no wise cast out" (John 6:37). The declaration of the gospel is lavishly displayed in the pages of Scripture, and

---

8. Van Til, *Common Grace*, 5. It should be added that the thought forms in apologetics that have influenced the present argument are heavily indebted to the work of Cornelius Van Til. See his *Christian Theory of Knowledge*, and *Defense of the Faith*.

the announcement is clear "Whosoever will may come." But the question presses, Who will? And the answer is that those will come whom God, by the regenerating grace of his Holy Spirit within them, has called to himself. The prophet Jeremiah spoke of those particular people half a millennium before the coming of Christ: "I have loved thee with an everlasting love; therefore with lovingkindness have I drawn thee" (Jer 31:3).

While it is to be said in such ways as we have observed that not all persons can come into the possession of the knowledge of God, it remains to observe, on the basis of such Scriptures as the apostle has stated in his letter to the Romans, that all individuals do, in fact and necessarily, have a cognition that God exists. The point is to be carefully recognized. By reason of his created status, there resides in the soul of every individual the innate consciousness that God exists and has a covenantal claim on man's worship and obedience. The apostle has put that in the following terms: "That which may be known of God is manifest in them; for God hath showed it unto them. For the invisible things of him from the creation of the world are clearly seen, being understood by the things that are made, even his eternal power and Godhead; so that they are without excuse" (Rom 1:19–20). But the difference in knowledge capacity must be clearly stated. Every man knows *that* God is. That is the burden of the scriptural data. But not every man knows *who* God is.

The question of the knowability of God calls also for at least a minimal recognition of a principal trend in thought that has influenced not only philosophy in general in its epistemological expression, but also the theological dogma of the church in latter times. I refer to the bequest of the late-Enlightenment philosopher already referred to, Immanuel Kant. For Kant's conclusion as to the knowledge of God has affected and tarnished many of the church's expressions on the level of theology proper, that is the doctrine of God and the knowability of God.

We drew attention in an earlier chapter to the two principal elements of Kantian thought that are now to be seen as relevant to his theological position and its influence on subsequent theological development. First, Kant argued that reality was to be understood as divided into two so-called realms: the phenomenal realm, the realm of things, or the perception of things, that could be seen and handled; and the noumenal realm, in which entities, genuine realities, might be thought possibly to exist. Knowledge, then, was confined or limited to what was observable in the phenomenal realm; or more particularly, it was confined to an individual's perception of what was existent in that realm. What might or might not exist in the noumenal realm was not knowable. For theology, Kant's critical step at that point was that he consigned God to the noumenal realm. God, Kant therefore said, might or might not exist. It was not possible to know.

The essence of Kant's argument, his position on the possible existence of God, can be indicated briefly. The upshot was that Kant argued that the existence of God could not be demonstrated as an element of "pure reason," but that it could conceivably be a usable, and even a necessary, assumption of "practical reason." In his *Critique of Practical Reason* he argued that "It is morally necessary to assume the existence of God [but] this moral necessity is subjective, that is, it is a want, and not objective."[9] That conclusion follows from Kant's earlier argument in his *Critique of Pure Reason*: "These remarks will have made it evident that the ideal of the Supreme Being, far from being an enouncement of the existence of a being in itself necessary, is nothing more than a regulative principle of reason . . . it exists merely in my own mind, as the formal condition of thought, but not as a material and hypostatic condition of existence."[10]

Kant's influence on doctrinal theology has continued to the present time in its liberal expressions, and the critical element has been that of the *un*knowability of God. But that very development has meant and implied that the ground of reason and knowledge is not to be found in the revelation that God has given, but in the assumption of the competence of unaided human reason. That, in a sentence, is the continuation, in many parts of contemporary theology, of what we have already identified as the pervasive assumption of human intellectual autonomy. It could be argued, if larger space were available at this time, that a corresponding assumption of the competence of unaided human reason informs certain evangelical apologetic arguments. The elevation of the virus of assumed autonomy in Kantian thought is clear in the second element we anticipated in Kant's epistemological philosophy. That is his argument regarding the processes of knowing, his so-called "Copernican revolution" in epistemology, but an examination of that level of thought is not necessary for our present purposes.

---

9. Kant, *Practical Reason*, 109.
10. Kant, *Pure Reason*, 306–307.

To know the thought of God

Our argument to this point has taken "the knowledge of God" in an objective sense, reflecting on God as the object of knowledge and addressing the question of whether it is possible for man to know God. We have concluded that it is possible, and, in fact, inescapable, for all men to know God in the sense of possessing at least a mere cognition of his existence. But beyond that, it is the high privilege of the regenerate man to know God as he has revealed himself, the God of grace who has made a revelation of himself and his purposes of redemption for sinners in the salvific work of his Son, the second Person of the Godhead, in this world. But we contemplated also that "the knowledge of God" may properly be understood in a subjective sense, meaning that the reference is to the knowledge that God himself possesses. Then the question arises as to whether it is possible for man to know what God knows; or to put the question in another way, whether the thoughts of God and the words of God are comprehensible to man, and if so, to what degree and in what sense. Those questions have given rise to a lot of spilled ink in the history of apologetic theology, and a minimal reference to the main points of interest, so far as they impinge on our present purposes, can be summarized as follows.

Two primary issues bear on our conclusions as to what is involved. First, we do well at the beginning to observe the statement of God as conveyed by the prophet Isaiah: "My thoughts are not your thoughts, neither are your ways my ways, saith the Lord. For as the heavens are higher than the earth, so are my ways higher than your ways, and my thoughts than your thoughts" (Isa 55:8–9). It may be asked whether that statement is to be understood in a primarily epistemological or a soteriological sense. If the former is in view, the statement carries the sense that the manner and method of knowing is different as between God and man. If a soteriological sense is in view, then the statement is saying that the way of salvation that God has provided is, in itself, vastly different from anything that man by his autonomous resources could have conjured or contemplated. Both those conclusions are, of course, true.

Second, it is necessary at this point to refer again to the state of man as he came from his Creator as the image of God, on the one hand, and as he exists in fallen state on the other. We have said that man is the image of God, and we adduce again the obvious conclusion that man thinks and speaks because God thinks and speaks. What is at issue is the manner, and the content, of the respective thinking and speaking. It is apposite to observe that when our first parent sinned and dragged all his posterity into sin, man did not cease to be the image of God (Gen 9:6; Jas 3:9). At the fall, the terms of the covenant of works that God has established and that placed certain obligations on man were not abrogated or abandoned. As the image of God, man continues to be liable for all the obligations of that covenant and will at last be judged on the basis of his having kept and fulfilled, or otherwise, those obligations. It is a proper and necessary statement of the gospel that the Son of God came into the world in order to do for his people what they were obligated to do under the covenant of works but what, because of their fallen state and captivity to sin, they could not do for themselves.

The ontological relation between God and man, we can now recall, is such that man as created is the analogue of God. He is the analogue of God as to his being and his knowledge. We observed previously that the important category of analogy required us to say that man is therefore *like* God but that he is not *identical* with God. At no point of our apologetic or our doctrinal construction do we give hospitality to the notion of the divinization of man. As to the level of being, man as the analogue of God exists because God exists and sustains him. As he came from the hands of his creator he was characterized, we have seen, by knowledge, holiness, and righteousness. Because he was the image of God that possession was an analogical knowledge, holiness, and righteousness.

Our interest now is with the category of knowledge. Consider, first, the possible relation between the words of God and the words of man as they may exist as a reflection, or repetition, of the words of God. If the words of God and the corresponding words of man have precisely at all points the same meaning and the same compass, we say that there is a "univocal" relation between them. They connote precisely and in all respects the same thing and they carry at all points the same exhaustive meaning. If, to take the opposite extreme, there was no correspondence at all between the words of God and the words of man we would say that the relation between them is not univocal, but "equivocal." In that case they carry no corresponding connotation. But, as we shall conclude, the relation between God's words and man's words is not univocal or equivocal, but "analogical." There is not, that is to say, a precise range of meaning between what God knows and what man can know in the analogical sense we have stated. The univocal-equivocal-analogical relations in theological statement were addressed, on the level of being, by Thomas Aquinas and were employed on the level of epistemology in Van Til's works we have referred to. Douglas

Kelly, in an interesting discussion of Aquinas and Duns Scotus, comments that the latter "argues that univocal being is a superior way to St. Thomas's assumption of analogical being between infinite and finite being."[11] The issues have recently been further addressed by Douglas Kelly, in, for example, his discussion of "Univocal epistemology" and its conceptual deficiencies.[12]

When we say that the range of meaning is different for man and God, we are simply drawing attention to the fact that, as the analogue of God, man, quite apart from the question of his regenerate or unregenerate status, exists in finitude and dependence and can only analogically reflect the infinitude of God. Let us take the following as an example of what is at issue. God and man, it may be supposed, both know that David was king of Israel. Is not the knowledge of God and that of man, therefore, precisely the same, and is not the relation between them univocal as a result? Our answer must be in the negative, because the range of meaning and implication is vastly different for the infinite God from what it is for man, who is the analogical creature of God. Further, and quite apart from the distinctive status of knowledge in the respective cases of God and man, it is equally clear that the process of knowledge is different in the two cases. For God, in his eternal creative activity and purpose knew all things in one eternal moment. Man, on the other hand, knows discursively and sequentially.

When we say that the relation between God and man on the level of knowledge is analogical, the question follows as to whether man can come into possession of "true" knowledge of God and the thoughts and words of God. Our answer is that man can and does acquire *true*, but not *comprehensive* knowledge of God. Let us put the conclusion in alternative terms. For that purpose, consider the fact that God has made a self-disclosure, a self-revelation and a revelation of his purposes to man. One of the relevant forms of revelation, we said, was what God has said in the Scriptures. But now, God has not made a full disclosure of his being and essence, implying that the Scriptures contain only a partial revelation of God. Moreover, the Scriptures as written contain only a partial record of what God has said to man and has done. John has said at the end of his gospel, for example, that "there are many other things which Jesus did, the which, if they should be written every one, even the world itself could not contain the books that should be written" (John 21:25). But it is to be acknowledged, further, that by reason that our cognitive and intellective capacities have been dulled by

---

11. Kelly, *Systematic Theology, Volume One*, 113.
12. Ibid., 358.

sin, it is possible for us to grasp only a part, and a partial understanding, of what the Scriptures contain. In the outcome, therefore, we can at best lay claim to only a partial comprehension of the partial revelation of God contained in the Scriptures, which themselves constitute only a partial record of what God has said and done.

The extent and quality of man's knowledge of God, and of the thoughts and words of God, can be addressed in another way. We reflect on the facts, or the constellations of facts, that God has revealed. We lay it down as a relevant epistemological proposition that it is the meaning of the fact that gives the fact its factness. Consider the following example. There was, on a certain occasion, a man who was nailed to a cross on Calvary's hill. His name was Jesus of Nazareth. He had gone about doing good, but the Jews had enlisted the aid of the Roman authorities in having him crucified because, among other things, he claimed himself to be God. We have before us, then, the phenomenon of a man dying on a cross. We may envisage two quite separate men observing that phenomenon, and we may ask quite simply what was the fact they respectively observed. One man, as he looked at the cross, and whom the Spirit of God had left completely untouched, saw a man dying, a deceiver and a blasphemer who was receiving the desserts of his misguided and misspent life. The other man, who had been the recipient of the regenerating grace of God, saw on the cross the Son of God dying as the substitute for sinners. Did the two men, we may ask, observe the same fact? Surely the answer to that question must be in the negative. The fact was different for one man from what it was for the other. In sharp focus, in other words, it was the meaning of the fact that established the fact for what it truly was.

Similarly, the Scriptures convey to us not only certain facts, facts relating to God's creation, providence, and redemptive purposes and accomplishment, but also the meaning of the facts. That, as in the case we have just noted, implies again that it is possible for man to come into the possession of a *true*, but nevertheless not a *comprehensive*, knowledge and understanding of the thoughts and the words of God.

That again throws its light on the relation between what it is that God thinks and knows and what man (to say again, existing as his analogue as to being and knowledge) thinks and knows. The knowledge that man himself is capable of knowing is, as has been said, an analogue of what God, in his infinity and eternity, knows and has said.

The free offer of the gospel

A highly significant implication for pastoral theology, for the preaching of the gospel and the ministry of the church in doing so, follows from what has been said to this point. The terms of the gospel, in all its gracious scope, its divine revelation, and its meaning for life and for eternity, does not call for extended articulation at this time. It is spelled out liberally on the pages of Scripture. The questions that follow from the apologetic statement we have made have to do with what is understood as the epistemic status, or the ability to receive the gospel, of those to whom it is presented.

We recall the conclusion that, in short, the regenerate individual *can* and *does* know God, but that the natural, unregenerate man *does not* and *cannot* know God. It is part of what exists as the epistemic antithesis between those two classes of individuals that raises the questions we now confront briefly. Two logical questions arise: first, whether, if what we have stated as the antithesis between the Christian believer and the non-believer exists, is there any point at all in offering the gospel to all and sundry individuals; and second, if grounds do exist on which the offer of the gospel can and should be made, how, as a result, are its terms, conditions, and promises to be presented?

The first of those questions raises the important issue, which has already been discussed at some length, of whether a "point of contact" exists between the epistemically darkened unregenerate person and the gospel as scripturally stated. We answer in the affirmative. Our answer turns on the fact that man is created as the image of God. A larger discussion at that point would require it to be said not that man *bears* the image of God, but that he *is* the image of God. That follows from what we discussed previously as the fact that man, as to both his being and his knowledge, is the analogue of God. The implications of that existential fact are stamped indelibly on the human soul. But the "point of contact" does not exist, and cannot be stated to exist, in the *imago Dei* as such. More particularly, the "point of contact" inheres in what is to be recognized as an aspect or implication of that image of God. That is that there exists in every person a *sensus deitatis*, an awareness of God from which there is no voluntary escape.

Granted, then, that the important "point of contact" we have recognized exists in the universal and unarguable "*sensus deitatis*," and not in any natural capacity or endowment, how, then, is the statement of the gospel affected? In short, the offer of the gospel cannot properly be made to any audience in a manner that is based on the assumption that the hearers possess a natural ability to receive it and to believe its content. The biblical data make it abundantly clear that the opposite is true. The assumption cannot be held that every man is naturally in possession of the capacity to believe and accept the gospel if only he sovereignly decides and agrees to do so. That way lies Pelagianism and its derivatives in such theological persuasions as Arminianism. It remains true, of course, that as the sovereign purpose of God may require, the statement of the gospel may carry with it its own convicting power. That is to say, the ministry or the Holy Spirit in the soul of the hearer may and, of course does in God's sovereignly declared instances, awaken and enlighten the hearer to receive it. As some theologians put it, truth carries with it its own potential deposit of faith.[13] But the gospel must not be stated in a manner that conveys the assumption that all men everywhere possess a natural ability to believe. On the level of evangelism, that is the reflection of the recognition, as we stated it on the level of apologetics, that there does not exist a reason-in-general in which the regenerate and the unregenerate share.

It is to be clearly stated that "Christ Jesus came into the world to save sinners" (1 Tim 1:15), and that if the hearer, in the light of what has now been explained to him, and if the Holy Spirit of God has called and enlightened him to see and know the truth, knows himself to be a sinner, then he may turn in belief and commitment to Christ and receive the assurance of sins forgiven. It is Christ who saves, by the work of his Holy Spirit, and not any assumed epistemic competence of the natural, unregenerate man.

Conclusion

We began by considering the possibility that man can know God. A full summary of what we have concluded is not necessary at this point. Suffice it to say three things:

First, it is necessary in submitting answers to the questions that arise, to formulate carefully what is understood as the object and the subject of knowledge respectively. If God and his words and thoughts are taken as the object of knowledge, the result is that man can have a true but not comprehensive knowledge, that knowledge at best being an analogy of what resides in the mind of God.

Second, it is a legitimate exercise on the part of man to reflect on the twofold possibilities of the knowledge process; firstly, as has just been said,

13. See the discussion on that point in Kelly, *Systematic Theology, Volume One*, 17–18.

on the extent to which, and the degree to which, man can have a knowledge of God as the object of knowledge; or, that is, to consider the extent to which man can know God. And secondly, to reflect on the manner in which, and the extent to which, what God himself as the subject of knowledge knows, and whether, in what form, and again to what extent and degree, that knowledge is communicable to man.

Third, man stands on all levels, that of being and that of knowledge, as the analogue of God. God in his simplicity, eternality, infinity, omniscience, and immutability, is the God of grace who has provided in his own Son a way by which sinners may be reconciled to himself. Those who, by divine decree, are the beneficiaries of the saving grace of God know him, partially in this world and prospectively to higher degree in the world to come. That, the absolute dependence of man on God, is the glory of the gospel of salvation.

Chapter 4

The Triune Redemption of the Church

THE PRINCIPAL CONCLUSION OF the argument in this chapter acknowledges that the divine objective in the covenantal formation of the church was the glorification throughout eternity of God the Son, the blessed Second Person of the Godhead. For "all things were created by him *and for him*" (Col 1:16). At this point we come to the principal conclusions regarding the evangel and its implied evangelism that we referred to in summary form in chapter 1. As anticipated there, emphasis will be laid on the humanness of Christ and the meaning of that for the death he suffered on the cross in the soulish aspect of his human nature. With that objective in view, it is necessary to focus thought on the participation of the triune Persons of the Godhead in the redemptive work that Christ accomplished. The "triune" in that statement aims to bring into perspective not only the trinitarian consubstantiality and the implied perichoresis, or the mutual indwelling, of the Persons of the Godhead. At issue also is the vastly important empirical fact that in the accomplishment and application of redemption the three persons of the Godhead are jointly engaged. That, moreover, is to be said of all of the works of God external to the Godhead, the divine *opera ad extra*.[1] While a fuller development of the doctrine of the trinity of the Godhead is beyond our present objective, that does stand in need of further and extended exploration at this time. John Owen, the seventeenth-century Puritan theologian, has pointed us to that task: "There is no grace whereby our souls go forth unto God, no act of divine worship yielded unto him, no

---

1. The relation between the being of God in perichoresis and the joint working of the Persons of the Trinity is explored informatively in Kelly, *Systematic Theology,* 453–55, 489–93.

duty of obedience performed, but they are distinctly directed unto Father, Son, and Spirit."[2]

It is a sound doctrinal habit to address the work of salvation primarily in terms of the redemptive office of God the Son, as that voluntarily-embraced assignment issued from the council of the Godhead before the foundation of the world. The terms of the eternally-stated covenant of redemption, and the distribution of redemptive offices that was inherent in it, are spread liberally on the pages of Scripture: The Father's election, the Son's substitutionary offering of himself in this world, and the Holy Spirit's application of redemption to those for whom Christ died. Christ came in covenantal assignment, as we shall see more fully in the following chapter, to "save his people from their sins" (Matt 1:21). His people, he was later to acknowledge to the Father, were those whom "thou gavest me" (John 17:6). In the particularity of the atonement that Christ came into the world to effect, he paid to the justice of God the "ransom" (Matt 20:28) that was necessary to reconcile his people to God. It follows that the implementation of the design of redemption engages explicitly the salvific work of God the Son incarnate.[3] Our concern, then, is to endeavor to understand primarily what is said within the compass of revelation of the identity and accomplishment in this world of God the Son. In saying that, we are acknowledging that our redeemer was not always Jesus Christ, but that he was, as he continued to be and remains, the Second Person of the Godhead who came into the world to *become* Jesus Christ for our redemption.

It is worth mentioning at the outset the following argument, in order to distance what follows from such sub-biblical theologies as draw a distinction between the works of God the Son and God the Holy Spirit. The essence of Arminianism at corresponding levels is to claim that whereas Christ died for all men indiscriminately, only those will be saved whom God foresees will accept the offer of salvation in Christ. That is, in the Arminian scheme Christ died for *all* men; but the Holy Spirit calls only *some* men (namely, those who sovereignly decide to believe in Christ). But such a conclusion drives a wedge between the *knowledge* possessed by Christ and the *knowledge* possessed by the Spirit. For our Lord had said "I lay down my life for the sheep" (John 10:15), and I know my own sheep "by name" (John 10:3). But if there is a wedge between the *knowledge* of the Son and

---

2. Owen, "Of Communion with God the Father, Son, and Holy Spirit," 2:15. See also the very valuable work by McGraw, *Knowing the Trinity*.

3. See Wellum, *God the Son Incarnate*.

the *knowledge* of the Holy Spirit, that in turn drives a wedge between the *Person* of Christ and the *Person* of the Holy Spirit. It follows, then, that such a conclusion destroys the simplicity of the Godhead, and that implies the destruction of the doctrine of God.

Moreover, if the Arminian scheme is adopted the best that could be said about the atonement of Christ is that he died in order to make salvation possible. But the Reformed doctrine that informs our study in no sense subscribes to such a possibility theory of salvation. Christ did not die in order to make salvation possible and dependent on sovereign human decisions. If that were the case, it would have to be said that in his death Christ did not really save anybody. All he accomplished was to make salvation possible. The biblical data, to the contrary, make it abundantly clear that in his death Christ actually saved his people.

But before the relevant doctrinal loci are addressed directly, we note briefly some of the scriptural data that bear on the theme that primarily engages us, the glory and the glorification of the Son of God. He is, as the letter to the Hebrews states it, "the brightness of [God's] glory and the express image of his person," who "upholds all things by the word of his power" (Heb 1:3), and whom "God . . . appointed heir of all things" (Heb 1:2). It is he who, being "in the bosom of the Father," came to "declare" God unto us (John 1:18), and who, when he was in this world, referred to himself as "the Son of man which is in heaven" (John 3:13, KJV).[4] In his high priestly prayer Christ prayed expressively: "Father . . . I have glorified thee on the earth. I have finished the work which thou gavest me to do. And now, O Father, glorify thou me with thine own self with the glory which I had with thee before the world was" (John 17:1, 4–5). And "being found in fashion as a man, he humbled himself, and became obedient unto death, even the death of the cross. Wherefore God also hath highly exalted him, and given him a name which is above every name, that at the name of Jesus every knee should bow . . . and that every tongue should confess that Jesus Christ is Lord, to the glory of God the Father" (Phil 2:8–11). He was, by his resurrection, "declared to be the Son of God with power" (Rom 1:4).[5] And now, in the heavens, "he shall see of the travail of his soul, and shall be satisfied" (Isa 53:11). The "travail of his soul," the results of the redemptive

---

4. It is well known that the last-mentioned phrase does not appear in some Greek manuscripts and therefore in translation. See the evaluation, summary, and argument for retention of the phrase as expressing a doctrinal truth in Hendriksen, *Commentary*, 2:500–501.

5. See the comment at that point by Murray, *Romans: Volume 1*, 10–12.

work he came to effect, is the church that he redeemed. He now looks with favor on his church, with pleasure and satisfaction. He, with the Father, is satisfied in the redemptive results and in the glory to which he has brought his redeemed church to be with himself. It is he who "loved the church and gave himself for it" (Eph 5:25), the church "which he purchased with his own blood" (Acts 20:28). The scriptural data could be multiplied and are substantially well known.

But leaving aside a more expansive review of the issues we have raised, we turn to a direct discussion of the Person and the work of Christ himself as he discharged his redemptive commission in the world. In doing so, we shall observe more briefly on the participation in that work of God the Father and God the Holy Spirit.

The incarnation of the Son of God

In the implementation in historic time of the terms of the covenant of redemption it is said that "when the fulness of the time was come, God sent forth his Son, made of a woman, made under the law, to redeem them that were under the law, that we might receive the adoption of sons" (Gal 4:4–5). Certain features related to that incarnation are to be noted carefully.

First, God did not at that time create a fetus for implantation in the womb of the virgin. Nor was the birth that resulted a natural parthenogenesis. Rather, it is of vital importance to observe that the birth of the Christchild resulted from the superintending power and work of the Holy Spirit, and it was such that the child was born of the *substance* of the mother. Thus he partook of genuine humanity. That is to say, at that point in time, at the point of fertilization in the virgin's womb, the Second Person of the eternal Godhead assumed to himself a true human nature. It is necessary, for purposes of the discussion that follows, to observe with some care what was involved in the conception and the birth of Jesus Christ at that time. We shall see that at a critical point in the early history of the church, notably at the Council of Chalcedon in the year 451 and the so-called christological settlement, the doctrine of the union of the two natures in Christ, the divine and the human, was brought to precise expression.

It follows that Jesus Christ, as he was in this world, possessed a true human nature with, as we shall see, all created faculties of human soul. That, there is reason to conclude, was brought to effect by the occurrence of two divine miracles, or, as it may be preferred to say, the conjunction of two aspects of the miracle that occurred. In the first place, the entailment of sin was broken, and the human nature that Christ assumed was a sinless human nature. That is in no sense to be attributed, as the errant doctrine of Rome argues, to the immaculate conception of the virgin mother, or, that is, to the supposition that she herself had been born free of the taint of original sin. As to what we have referred to as the breaking of the entailment of sin, we note the announcement of the angel Gabriel to the mother: "The Holy Ghost shall come upon thee, and the power of the Highest shall overshadow thee; therefore also the *holy thing* which shall be born of thee shall be called the Son of God" (Luke 1:35). It was not being said at that point that the child to be born would, on that account and at that time, be adopted as the Son of God. We distance our christological doctrine from the early heresies of adoptionism. What was being stated by the angel was that the eternal Son of God would enter into time and assume human nature in the act of doing so. It was the Son of God who would be born in the manger.

Clearly involved at that point is the joint working of the divine triune Persons of the Godhead, as we anticipated at the beginning. God the Father sent the Holy Spirit in active participation in the incarnation of God the Son. The old Puritan commentator, Matthew Poole, has observed on the point in hand: "This phrase ['the power of the highest shall overshadow thee'] denoteth an extraordinary special influence of the Spirit, *changing the order and course of nature*."[6] And Calvin, having observed that in the incarnation of Christ "The operation of the Spirit would be secret, as if an intervening cloud did not permit it to be beheld by the eyes of men, concludes that "Though Christ was formed of the seed of Abraham, yet he contracted no defilement from a sinful nature; for the Spirit of God kept him pure from the very commencement. . . . The manner of conception, therefore, assures us that we have a Mediator *separate from sinners*" (Heb 7: 26).[7]

The first aspect of miracle at the incarnation was thus the breaking of the entailment of sin. The second was, as has been seen, the fertilization of the egg of the virgin by the action of the Holy Spirit.

In the ways we have examined, there appeared in this world a divine Person, the Second Person of the Godhead, who was in full possession of both a divine nature and a human nature. Before we reflect on the manner in which the early church formed and consolidated its dogma on the

---

6. Poole, *Commentary*, 190, italics added.
7. Calvin, *Commentary* on *Harmony*, 42–44.

Personhood of Jesus Christ, we note certain necessary characteristics of the human nature that was assumed. That is to say, Jesus Christ possessed a human nature, in both body and soul, that was characterized by the full and ordinary human faculties of soul, intellect, emotion, and will, yet without sin. We say only at this point by way of anticipation that those realities of soul were and remained crucially relevant, not only to Christ's actions in this world, but also to his death on the cross.

With that in view and for purposes of what lies ahead, it is relevant to ask more particularly what is involved in the meaning of humanness, or humanity, or what is involved in human nature. It might be said, most usually and of course significantly, that human nature is such that the human person possesses both a body and a soul. But it is suggested that care should be taken in definition and explanation at that point. For if it is said in that way that man possesses both a body and a soul, then three entities are in view—first the individual about whom the statement is being made; second, the body that he has; and third, the soul that he has. It may well be more meaningful to let the focus of our answer fall on the unity and singularity of personhood and say that the *person* is characterized by *human nature* in its *bodily aspect* and in its *soulish aspect*. That being so, certain human performances must clearly be referable to actions directly attributable to the capacities of the *bodily aspect* of a person, and correspondingly, certain performances are attributable to the *soulish aspect*. In that way, the reality of integral personhood is preserved, along with, it is important to note, the responsibility and accountability of the person. For to take, for example, the instance of human sin, whether actions of sin are immediately referable to the bodily aspect or the soulish aspect, it is the *person* who sins and who is responsible for sin.

In that connection, a statement of singular significance occurs in Paul's letter to the Romans at Romans 6:6, "Our old man is crucified with him [Christ] that the body of sin might be destroyed." The meaning of "the body of sin" at that point has been variously understood. Some, for example Calvin, understand the reference to be to a mass of sin that resides in the person. Others, for example John Murray, understand the reference to be to the actual human body "as conditioned and controlled by sin."[8] Murray sees the body, that is, as "an integral part of personality."[9] In that perspective, then, the bodily aspect of personhood is brought into view and emphasis.

---

8. See the discussion in Murray, *Romans*, 220.
9. Ibid., 221.

Those conclusions will be seen to be relevant to the Person and the redemptive work of our Lord. But it is of serious moment to note in that connection that there arose in the early church certain heresies that contradicted what has just been said regarding the twofold natures of Jesus Christ. The general character of those heresies is important for what must be observed as their essential intent. For if, in the various ways we shall note, the true personhood of Christ could be destroyed, then the new religion of Christianity would fall to the ground. It is possible to have, for example, Aristotelian philosophy without Aristotle, or Marxism without Marx. It is possible for a system of thought to survive beyond the death of its originator, the identity of whom does not remain integral with the perseverance of the thought system itself. But it is not possible to have Christianity without Christ. General histories of theological doctrine expand on the heresies of *Apollinarism* (that Christ was a divine spiritual being who did not take to himself a true human nature, essentially appearing in a human body but without a human soul); *Arianism* (Christ was a created being and not eternally God and consubstantial with the Father and the Holy Spirit); *Sabellianism* (Christ and the Holy Spirit were emanations of, or modes of being of, God, but were not distinguishable persons); *Eutychianism* (Christ's human nature was absorbed into his divine nature, and Christ existed in the world in only that one divine nature); *Nestorianism* (Christ's two natures existed as essentially two persons). Those heresies were addressed in four councils of the church: *Nicea* (325), *Constantinople* (381), *Ephesus* (431), *Chalcedon* (451).

For our present purposes, it is the deliverance of the Council of Chalcedon that assumes importance. For what was stated there became accepted by the church as the definitive dogma on the personhood of Christ. It was concluded at Chalcedon that the Second Person of the Godhead, appearing in this world in the manner we have stated, took to himself in union with his divine nature a true human nature (that occurred, as we have seen, at the incarnation) such that the two natures were joined "without confusion, without change, without division, and without separation." The first two of those defining characteristics mean that there was no communication of properties between the two natures. The divine remained divine without any admixture to, or in, of any properties of the human nature. Again, the human nature remained completely human without any admixture of, or from, the divine nature. The last two of the defining characteristics meant that the union of natures was a real union. It will be observed that the personhood of Christ remained such as came into being by the union of natures that we have observed and that now, in heaven, Christ continues to exist in the same union of divine and human natures.

We recall at this point our previous statement regarding Christ's being in heaven while he was in this world. It can now be stated that while he was in this world, as to his human nature he was, as stated, in the world, but as to his divine nature he was both in this world and in heaven. Now, it can be correspondingly stated, as to his human nature Christ is in heaven, but as to his divine nature he is both in this world and in heaven. We are saying, that is, that in this world Jesus Christ was not a human person. He was, and he remained, a divine Person. Now that he has ascended to heaven and has assumed a bodily form appropriate to his existence in eternal spiritual (pneumatic) state (corresponding to the body his saints will assume appropriate to their existence in eternal spiritual state) Christ has not divested himself of his true humanity. We can sum up by saying that at the incarnation Christ took into union with his divine nature a created (by the manner we have indicated), finite, and temporal human nature. He continues now for all eternity in that created, finite, and temporal human nature. What a remarkable fact and revelation that the One who had created time should enter into time, and should continue in temporal state, for our redemption! For the essence of the meaning of time is that it is "God-created as a mode of finite existence."[10]

Implicit in our conclusion regarding the personhood of Christ is the fact that there existed in him two minds, a divine and a human, two capacities for affection, a divine and a human, and both a divine and a human will. It was one of the early heresies, *monothelitism*, to argue that Christ possessed only one will. As to his personhood, then, we say that the locus of his personhood was in his divine nature. The state of the faculties of soul, the human mind and the human will for example, describes the *nature* of the soul, while the *person* is the entity that lives and functions responsibly and consistently with that nature. Jesus Christ, that is to say, is the Person who, in certain situations and at certain times, acted in and through his human nature, and also, at certain times and in certain situations, acted in and through his divine nature. In the former, we say, recalling our comments on the meaning of personhood and human nature, that certain actions of our Lord were directly attributable to, respectively, the *bodily aspect* ("Jesus wept," John 11:35; "he hungered," Luke 4:2) and the *soulish aspect* ("my soul

---

10. Van Til, *Introduction to Systematic Theology*, 66.

is exceeding sorrowful," Matt 26:38) of his personhood. More particularly, as we shall go on to see, our Lord, who died in his human nature, suffered on the cross in the soulish aspect of that nature (in his cry of derelicition) and in the bodily aspect (in his temporal death).

Our doctrine of the personhood of Christ, with reference now to his divine nature, is in no sense kenotic. That is, he did not lay aside in this world any aspect of his eternal glory, though he did, of course, lay aside the signs and insignia of his glory.[11] He remained, in his divine nature, in possession of all of the divine attributes of omnipresence, omniscience, and omnipotence.

The covenantal obedience of Christ

It follows from our introductory comment on the origination of the redemptive office of Christ in the council of the Godhead before the foundation of the world that his obedience to that office and his redemptive accomplishment are to be understood in covenantal terms.[12] If the objectives of the determinate covenant of redemption were to be realized, it was necessary that what can be conceived of as an implementing covenant should come into effect for that purpose. God the Father elected to reconcile to himself a defined and unalterable number of persons from among the fallen sons of Adam,[13] and having given them to his Son that he might do all that was necessary to their salvation, there came into being for that purpose a covenant of grace. That was a conditional covenant in a profound respect. The parties to the covenant were God the Father on the one hand and his elect people on the other. Or it may be said that the respective parties were God and his chosen people as represented by Christ. The covenant was not conditional on the part of the subjects of it, the people defined as the beneficiaries of it. As to their status and potentialities, the covenant was unconditional because all the provision for its fulfillment was made by the grace of God. "By grace are ye saved," the apostle explained to the

---

11. Kenoticism relies on a misreading of the text at Philippians 2:7, where the verb "ekenosen" means "emptied."

12. We shall return to an extended discussion of God's covenants in the following chapter.

13. That statement implies an infralapsarian view of God's electing grace. The larger exposition of that assumption and the different proposal of supralapsarianism does not detain us at this time.

Ephesians (Eph 2:5, 8). But the condition attached to the covenant lay on Christ, the party to it on behalf of his people. For in order for the realization of the designated ends, the covenant was conditional on Christ's faithful and complete fulfillment of its terms and requirements.

Christ, that is, voluntarily took on himself the responsibility to act in every necessary respect as the salvific substitute for the people whom he represented. His discharge of all of the relevant obligations was punctilious, impeccable, and complete. The apostle in his letter to the Romans has summed up the matter in a remarkable paragraph that sets side by side and distinguishes the headship of the first Adam, by whose sin we were all dragged down into a state of sin and estrangement from God, and that of the second Adam, Jesus Christ our redeemer. "As by one man's [Adam's] disobedience many were made sinners, so by the obedience of one [Jesus Christ] shall many be made righteous" (Rom 5:19). Before us now, therefore, is the question of how that divinely-declared objective was accomplished.

At that point, it is necessary to bring back to perspective what has already been said regarding the human nature of Christ. While that is so we recall, for minimal repetition, that all of the actions we are about to consider were actions of the *Person* of Jesus Christ. Some of those actions were, it can be clearly established, immediately attributable to our Lord's human nature. But we avoid doctrinal error and confusion by insisting that those actions were the actions of the *Person* of Christ. Actions by the *Person* of Christ, that is to say, were actions in and through his divine or his human natures respectively. And while, as has been seen, there was no communication of properties between the two natures there was, as became necessary, a communication of knowledge and information between the respective minds.

We look, first, at what has been referred to as Christ's "active obedience." By that we mean his perfect fulfillment of the law of God from which his chosen people had derogated and which they had failed to fulfill. It was necessary, in short, that in order for reconciliation with God to be effected a twofold requirement must be met. First, the law that God had promulgated must be honored and kept, and second, the penalty for having broken the law must be paid. In his comprehensive obedience, Christ met both those requirements on behalf of his people. We have just referred to Christ's substitutionary keeping the law as his active obedience. But there was, of course, a passive element of that active obedience. That was our Lord's voluntarily submitting himself to the will of the Father. "I came down from heaven," he said, "not to do mine own will, but the will of him that sent me" (John 6:38).

We refer also to Christ's "passive obedience," meaning by that his suffering on the cross in giving his life for the ransom of his people. That will engage us at length in a moment. But we say also that there was an element of active obedience in that passive obedience. For, as will be seen, Christ actively and at his own determination and volition laid down his life.

The atonement

It is necessary at this point to give attention to what can properly be referred to as the *qualification* of our Lord for the substitutionary, salvific actions he undertook. We have referred to the active obedience of Christ. That involved, as the letter to the Hebrews states it, his suffering for us, in various ways that are discoverable in the scriptural data, in order that he might be made "perfect through suffering" (Heb 2:10). Now it was that "suffering," and our Lord's ready devotion of himself to it, that *qualified* him to continue to discharge all of the requirements of his priestly office. The late-twentieth-century theologian and commentator, Philip Edgcumbe Hughes, has seen the point clearly: "It is fitting that our Redeemer should have been made *perfect through suffering*: first, because his completely victorious suffering of temptation of every kind (Heb 4:15) was essential to his achievement of that perfection which *qualified him* to offer himself on the cross as the spotless lamb of God in the place of sinners."[14]

What, then, are we to say of our Lord's actual suffering on the cross when he laid down his life for his people? To see the meaning and significance of that in full perspective it is necessary to acknowledge briefly two preceding features of his substitutionary offering.

First, consider the divine transaction that occurred on the cross. We adduce for that purpose the apostle's explanation: "For [God] hath made him to be sin for us, who knew no sin, that we might be made the righteousness of God in him" (2 Cor 5:21). In short, on the cross, the guilt of our sin was imputed to Christ, or was placed to his account, in order that by reciprocal imputation his righteousness might be placed to our account. That statement from 2 Corinthians 5:21 states clearly that the latter proceeds from, in the sense that it is dependent on, the achieved righteousness of Christ. That follows, in the context of reciprocal imputation, because the

---

14. Hughes, *Hebrews*, 100, italics added.

perfect obedience that Christ offered to the demands of the law included the legal act of his dying on the sinner's behalf. By that it is meant that in a significant sense Christ's act of dying was itself obedience to law. For the law said that the guilty must die (Ezek 18:4, 20). In, then, Christ's submission to that requirement, submission, that is, in bearing the guilt of sin as our substitute, we see his final act of active obedience.

But the terms of the great exchange involved in what we have recognized as reciprocal imputation have not always been clearly understood or stated. When we refer to "guilt," we do not have in view any such subjective notion as the unease of feeling that we may experience because of our default in a particular direction or matter. What is involved is not the subjective, but the objective unworthiness that characterizes us because we have not met the requirements of the law of God. We hold to the grand objectivity of the exchange referred to. For the essence of the meaning of "guilt" as now referred to is that guilt is unfulfilled obligation. But it is necessary to distinguish between what *was* thus imputed to Christ and what was *not* imputed to him. What was imputed was the sinner's guilt. What was not imputed was the sinner's sinful state. If the latter had been done, then Christ on the cross would have been made a sinner. We ask, was he guilty? And we answer "Yes." But he was guilty, not of his own sin, for he was in every respect sinless, but of the sin of his people for whom he died.

It is unfortunately true that even in purportedly Reformed theological circles confusion and misleading errors on that critically important matter have occurred. Michael Horton, for example, argues with reference to what he terms the "marvelous exchange," that "Jesus Christ, sinless in himself, became the greatest sinner who ever lived."[15] Horton's statement reproduces the similar conclusion of Martin Luther in his comment on Galatians 3:13: "Christ [became] the greatest transgressor, murderer, adulterer, thief, rebel, blasphemer . . . that ever was or could be in all the world."[16] In commenting that "Christ was made a curse for us," Luther concludes, in what we may judge as a *non sequitur*, that "If it is not absurd to confess and believe that Christ was crucified between two thieves, then it is not absurd to say also that he was accursed and of all sinners the greatest."[17] Christ was constituted guilty, but he was not constituted a sinner. Philip Hughes has again seen this important aspect of the atonement clearly: "God, declares Paul, made the Sinless One

---

15. Horton, *Christian* Faith, 621.
16. Luther, *Galatians*, 269.
17. Ibid., 270.

sin for us. It is important to notice that he does not say that God made Him a *sinner*; for to conceive of Christ as sinful, or made a sinner, would be to overthrow the very foundation of redemption, which demands the death of an altogether Sinless One in the place of sinful mankind."[18]

What was involved in the imputation of Christ's righteousness to the sinner again calls for careful formulation. For the righteousness of Christ that is placed to the sinner's account is the *forensic* righteousness of Christ. "Forensic" means "in relation to law." And what is at issue at this point is that the forensic righteousness of Christ is the righteousness that accrued to him by reason that he was in complete obedience to the law of God. What was *not* imputed to the sinner was the *essential* righteousness of Christ, meaning by that that the sinner for whom Christ died did not, on that account, become a partaker of the essence of God, or become a little God. We avoid at every turn any suggestion of the divinization of man.

When we focus in that way on the *forensic* righteousness of Christ, the import of the apostle's statement in his letter to the Romans comes clearly into view. "In due time Christ died for the ungodly" (Rom 5:6). At the point at which the sinner stands at the cross of Christ in repentance and saving faith, he is ungodly, meaning by that that he has failed to keep the law of God. But at that point God declares that the sinner who stands before him ungodly is, in fact, now regarded by God as godly. That can be so, because, as has been seen, God places to that sinner's account the forensic righteousness of Christ. John Murray has clarified the relations involved in the following terms: "Justification is a constitutive act, not barely declarative."[19] Justification is God's declarative, forensic statement that the sinner is now regarded as righteous. But in order for God truthfully to *declare* the sinner righteous, that sinner must actually *be* righteous. God therefore *constitutes* the sinner righteous by imputing Christ's forensic righteousness to him in the manner we have seen. Correspondingly, God cannot truthfully *declare* Christ guilty unless he *is*, in fact, guilty. God therefore *constitutes* Christ guilty by imputing to him the guilt of the sinner. By that transaction on the cross, and by the reciprocal imputation that is involved, God now looks on the repentant sinner as though he himself had kept the law, and as though he himself has paid the penalty for having broken the law.

---

18. Hughes, *Corinthians*, 213.
19. Murray, *Romans*, 206.

The participation of the divine Persons

The second matter preliminary to understanding the divine transaction on the cross takes up our observation at the beginning that in all the works of God external to the Godhead the three Persons of the Godhead are jointly engaged. We observed the presence of the three Persons of the Godhead at the incarnation of our Lord. Christ said that he came to reveal the Father and said to Philip that "he that hath seen me hath seen the Father" (John 14:9), and "the words that I speak unto you I speak not of myself; but the Father that dwelleth in me, he doeth the works" (John 14:10). "The word which ye hear is not mine but the Father's which sent me" (John 14:24). At John 14:26, the Father sends the Holy Spirit, but he does so in the name of Christ. Christ speaks the words and the Holy Spirit conveys the meaning of them to the individual.

We have already seen Christ's declaration that he came to do the will of the Father who sent him. In his mission in this world it was our Lord's objective to reveal the glory of the Father, by declaring, and exhibiting in his words and works the Father's infinite perfections. But of immediate interest are two further respects in which the Persons of the Godhead are shown to have been active in the work of Christ.

Consider the presence of the Holy Spirit in Christ's work in this world. It must properly be said that all that Christ did in this world he did in the strength of the Holy Spirit. We have it in John 3:34 that "God giveth not the Spirit by measure unto him." And consider the presence of God the Father in the spoken voice, and the Holy Spirit's appearance in the form of a dove, on the occasion of our Lord's submission to the baptism of John. But of singular relevance is the statement of the Holy Spirit's presence that takes us to the cross of Christ and his sacrifice on our behalf. We have it clearly stated that it was "through the eternal Spirit" (Heb 9:14) that he offered himself. That it was again in the strength of the Holy Spirit that Christ offered himself demands deeper consideration.

That consideration makes it necessary to bring back to relevance what has been said regarding the Person of Christ in that he possessed a full human nature, with full faculties of human soul. Now it is clear that it was in that human nature that Christ died. He could not die in his eternal, divine nature. But again, we must invoke the reality, mysterious to the deepest degree that it is, that in all of the actions of Christ in this world, actions immediately attributable to his human nature on the one hand or to his divine nature on the other, those actions in their totality must be seen to be attributable to the *Person* of Christ. We have already submitted that argument at sufficient length. But we recognize at this point the fact that though, as has been said, the death of Christ is immediately attributable to his human nature (because he must pay the penalty for the sins of fallen human nature in *his* human nature) nevertheless it was the *Person* of Christ who died in that human nature. Paul the apostle made that point clearly when he stated that the Jews acted in ignorance when they crucified Christ, "which none of the princes of this world knew, for had they known it they would not have crucified the Lord of glory" (1 Cor 2:8). It was the Lord of glory, the *Person* of Jesus Christ, who died in his human nature.

It is important to recall, then, what has already been said regarding that human nature. That nature involves Christ's possession of "a true body and a reasonable soul."[20] The critical point to be taken into account, therefore, is that given, as the scriptural data copiously declare, that Christ suffered and died in his human nature, that suffering on the cross involved the suffering of human soul, in, that is, the human *soulish aspect* of his personhood, as well as his suffering of human *bodily aspect*. Certainly, as we shall see, Christ laid down his life in human death, in what we shall refer to as his temporal death, and the shedding of his blood at that point has immeasurable significance in the scriptural report and our interpretation of it. For it is clear that "without the shedding of blood there is no forgiveness of sins" (Heb 9:22, ESV). The shedding of blood was, of course, a critical feature of the Old Testament anticipations of the coming and the work of Christ. But it would be incorrect to say that the blood of Christ was shed simply because it was necessary in order to reflect in the antitype (the sacrifice of Christ) the Old Testament type (the blood of the bulls and goats). As we have observed in a previous context, the truth is the precise opposite. The blood of the animals was necessary because it had been foreordained from before the foundation of the world that the blood of Christ would be shed in effecting the salvation of his people, the promised Messiah dying in *his* human nature for the guilt of the sins of his people in *their* human nature. The biblical references to the blood of Christ, therefore, are properly to be understood as a synecdochical pointing to the sacrifice of Christ in its full compass and meaning.[21]

---

20. See *Westminster Shorter Catechism*, Question 22.

21. Bonar, in his valuable *Commentary on Leviticus*, 19–20, has drawn attention to the anticipation of the point made in the preceding paragraph by the requirements of the typical burnt offerings. "The priests shall lay the parts, the head, and the fat, in order . . . upon the altar:" (Lev 1:8). Bonar observes: "The *head* and this *fat* are two pieces—one *outward*, and the other *inward*; thus representing the whole *inner and outer man*. Christ's

It is apposite now to recall what has been said of the sacrificial death of Jesus Christ at the very beginning of these studies. Christ's suffering of soul on the cross is to be understood in terms of his cry of dereliction. Two things are to be recognized in relation to it. First, the transaction between the Father and the Son in that crucial hour was such that in his human soul our Savior passed through the pains of hell on our account. The suffering of human soul that was involved was in every respect substitutionary for the pains of eternal perdition that had properly accrued to us. But in that precise hour Christ conquered death for us. He had prayed "with strong crying and tears unto him that was able to save him from death, *and was heard* in that he feared" (Heb 5:7, italics added). It is to be noted that Christ did not pray to be saved from dying. He came into the world to die. "He was heard," as the text says, and he was saved from death. What is at issue in that profoundly significant statement is that as he passed through the pains of hell and confronted the devil and death, he was not overcome by death. He was, and he remained, in control of that awful process. Death did not overcome him. He overcame death. And while he tasted death for us, he conquered death and emerged from that encounter victorious. Therein lies the foundation and guarantee of our salvation and reconciliation with God.

But secondly, all that has just been said was possible because it was "through the eternal Spirit" that our Lord offered himself (Heb 9:14). Coming to focus, therefore, is, as has been anticipated, the conjunction of the Holy Spirit in that ultimate substitutionary work of Christ. Given that he died in his human nature, the Holy Spirit supported that nature in order that our Lord would sustain his total control over the forces and the onslaught of death and would be victorious. As the *Westminster Larger Catechism* states it, "It was requisite that the Mediator should be God, that he might sustain and keep the human nature from sinking under the infinite wrath of God."[22] There, in its highest and ultimate degree, is the fact that in the works of God external to the Godhead the three Persons of the Godhead are engaged. We see, on careful reflection, the engagement of the Father, the Son, and the Holy Spirit in the darkest hour of atonement that was effected in the death of Christ.

That Christ was in control of all of the processes of his offering on the cross, and that he was victorious over the claims of death, has been stated by an old Scottish theologian in sublime words that bear extended

---

whole manhood, *body and soul*, was placed on the altar, in the fire, and endured the wrath of God."

22. *Westminster Larger Catechism*, Question 38.

statement: "Will He not, in quiet patience, submit; and fall a victim unrelenting? . . . No: no. Jesus prevails to suffer all the tortures of man, and all the shafts of Satan, and all the strokes of His Father's sword—and behold! In His hour of chiefest weakness, He is strong to bear them all. His own activity is not overborne, and laid to rest, and in abeyance. He is the livingly active and triumphant Saviour still. Weak man, he sets far aside from Him. Baffled Satan, He banishes back to his place of darkness. His Father's wrath, He bears it all; exhausting in His afflicted soul the vials of all His curse. He passed through the hour and power of darkness unsubdued."[23]

Thus our Lord passed through eternal death. In his victory at that point he was *qualified* to then lay down his life in his temporal death. Hugh Martin again puts the remaining events of the cross before us: "With the cry of triumph on His parched but powerful lips; and His Father's light and love shed abroad again in His faithful heart; and the joy set before Him . . . as a Son, crying, Abba, Father, and committing His spirit [his human soul] to His Father's hands—even thus the conqueror livingly dies; by His own prevailing act, lays down His life for the sheep, a ransom; offers Himself to God, a sacrifice."[24] In that final act on the cross our Lord, voluntarily and at the moment of his choosing, laid down his life in his temporal death. For as he had made plain in his remarkable discourse on his identity as the good shepherd, "I lay down my life . . . no man taketh it from me, but I lay it down of myself. I have power to lay it down, and I have power to take it again" (John 10:17–18).

Conclusion

The principal questions we have addressed in the foregoing are, first, the cooperation, or joint engagement in the work of redemption of the three Persons of the Godhead. That joint engagement was observed at the incarnation of Christ, at the baptism of Christ, at the spiritual endowment of Christ, and finally at the atonement that Christ offered. His statement in his Supper Discourses on the night on which he was betrayed is apposite when he refers to "the *Holy Spirit* whom the *Father* will send *in my name*" (John 14:26). John Calvin states in his discussion of "Threeness": "Scripture sets forth a distinction of the Father from the Word, and of the Word from the Spirit. . .That passage from Gregory of Nazianzus vastly delights me: 'I cannot think of the one without quickly being encircled by the splendor of the three; nor can I

---

23. Martin, *The Abiding Presence*, 136.
24. Ibid., 137.

discern the three without being straightway carried back to the one."[25] Calvin, of course, goes on to speak of the distinction of offices of the respective Persons of the Godhead, and he rigorously avoids all possibility of errors, such as that of Patripassianism that troubled the church in earlier years.[26]

Second, the human nature of Christ was explored preparatory to adducing the significance of that human nature in the death of Christ on the sinner's behalf. Third, together with a recognition of the supportive accompaniment of the Holy Spirit in the suffering of Christ on the cross, the examination of the victory that Christ accomplished aimed to bring into focus the meaning of his passing through eternal death on the one hand and his temporal death on the other.

In the ways we have now examined, we observe the respects in which Jesus Christ, in this world in both divine and human natures, was alone qualified to perform all that was necessary to the salvation of his people, to, we may say, our eternal bliss and joy. First, we have seen that his suffering in his active obedience *qualified him* to go on to discharge all of the necessities of his high priestly office and function. Second, we have now seen that his passing victoriously through eternal death on the cross *qualified him* to go on to his temporal death that was necessary to the full payment of the penalty of our sin. For it was after he had conquered eternal death for us that he could say "It is finished" (John 19:30). In complete victory over hell and death, and in full satisfaction of all that was necessary to reconcile his people to God, he rose again from the dead, and in his resurrection he was "declared to be the Son of God with power" (Rom 1:4). Third, all that has been said of his victory *qualified him* to reign eternally as the Head of the church he had redeemed.

---

25. Calvin, *Institutes*, 141.

26. The Patripassians argued that there is only one divine Person, in eternity denominated as God the Father, but that in the incarnation as God the Son that divine Person animated the human body of Christ, but denying the existence of a true human soul in the Person of Jesus Christ. The implication was that the divine essence suffered for the sins of mankind. See Shedd, *History*, Vol. 1, 254–55.

Chapter 5

Covenantal Justification

AT SEVERAL POINTS OF the preceding chapters it was observed that Christ's coming into the world was in accordance with certain covenantal designs and arrangements. We have referred to the covenant of redemption that before the foundation of the world established redemptive offices of God the Father, God the Son, and God the Holy Spirit. A preliminary observation was made that for purposes of achieving its stated objectives that redemptive covenant between the Persons of the Godhead gave rise to a covenant of grace. It is necessary now to consider in somewhat more comprehensive terms the covenantal structure of the redemptive process and its accomplishment, and to consider the resulting benefits to those for whom Christ died. For that purpose, it will be profitable to reflect on the justification of those who, by the effectual call of God, receive God's declarative, forensic statement of justification as they stand, in God-given repentance and faith, at the cross of Christ and submit to him.

That objective can be realized most profitably by taking as our ordering principle the following sentence from the *Westminster Confession of Faith*, the seventeenth-century confession that has become the subsidiary doctrinal standards of Reformed churches: "The principal acts of saving faith are *accepting, receiving, and resting upon Christ alone for justification, sanctification, and eternal life*, by virtue of the *covenant of grace*."[1]

The italicized phrases in that statement indicate the essential relationship that should be prominent in the statement of the evangel. First, saving faith is a matter of "accepting, receiving, and resting on Christ alone."

---

1. *Westminster Confession of Faith*, XIV:2, italics added. Similar statements occur in the *Savoy Declaration of Faith* and the *Second London (Baptist) Confession*.

Second, the end in view as the benefit that follows saving faith is "justification, sanctification, and eternal life." And third, both the end in view and the means to that end are "by virtue of the covenant of grace."

The divine intentions of the covenant of grace led uninterruptedly to the cross of Christ. The death of Christ on the cross, tragic as it was, was not a catastrophe for which no reason existed or was to be found. It was not merely a random episode, a blip on the course of history that could, when it occurred, be shunted aside as the lives of men and nations moved on. On the cross of Christ, the Son of God, with a deliberateness born of divine counsel, died in the place of sinners. The apostle Peter on the Day of Pentecost stated to the "men of Israel" that they had "by wicked hands crucified and slain" one who was "delivered by the determinate counsel and foreknowledge of God" (Acts 2:22–23).

It was true that the people on that day did not know what they were doing. For as the apostle Paul was later to say, "none of the princes of this world," not Caiaphas or Pontius Pilate or the leaders of Israel, or, for that matter, the common people, had sufficient understanding to know that they were crucifying the Lord of glory. For as Paul said, "had they known it [had they known that it was the long-promised Messiah they were crucifying], they would not have crucified the Lord of glory" (1 Cor 2:8). The death of Christ was, on the level of its actual occurrence, an act of ignorance. But the ignorance, though it was sincere, was culpable. Christ had come "unto his own, and his own received him not" (John 1:11), because their eyes were blinded and they could not see.

That the death of Christ occurred in accordance with divine counsel, that it fulfilled the terms of the covenant of grace, is stated quite clearly in the seventeenth-century confessions of faith. Those confessions strike to the heart of what encapsulates the significance of the cross of Christ. That is that by repentance, faith, and trust in Christ the believing sinner is justified from his sin and enters into a new life in union with Christ. The Confessions at the point indicated, we have seen, are saying two things. First, those acts of saving faith ("accepting, receiving, and resting upon Christ") have efficacy for the objectives they realize ("justification, sanctification, and eternal life") only by reason of the benefits accruing from "the covenant of grace." Then it follows, secondly, that both the acts themselves and the objectives they realize are what they are because they were foreordained in the divine formulation of the covenant of grace.

We may state that second conclusion in other terms. It is not only that the covenant of grace contemplated the *ends* and *objectives* that have been stated. But the very *means*, the acts themselves that conduce to those ends, have been foreordained as elements of the covenant of grace. Every instance of individual saving faith is itself foreordained as an integral aspect of that covenant. What that is saying is that salvation in all its parts is by the grace of God. It destroys every suggestion that salvation is an autosoterism on an individual's part on the one hand, or a divine-human synergism on the other. Against the autosoterism of the Pelagians and the synergism in the semi-Pelagianism of Rome, the gospel insists that salvation is a divine monergism.[2]

If, then, the doctrines of salvation and the Christian life are to be biblically-consistent they must also find their grounding in the biblical doctrine of the covenant. It is for that reason that Reformed theology has been properly described as covenant theology. The reality and the meaning of God's covenantal purpose provide the fundamental hermeneutical principle in terms of which we hear the Scriptures speak. By that we mean that when we marshal our understanding of the acts of salvation under the heading of the *ordo salutis* (the statement of the order of application of redemption) each of those acts is to be seen as covenantally grounded and warranted. In the present instance of saving faith and justification, God's declarative-forensic statement of justification is what it is, it conveys its peculiar significance to those who are the beneficiaries of it, and it sustains its relation to all of the saving acts of God because its occurrence and import are vital aspects

---

2. Pelagius was a British monk who claimed that the faculties of the soul had not been subject to depravity as a result of Adam's fall in the manner we shall go on to explore. He argued, as Harnack in his *Outlines,* 370, observes, that "All men stand in the condition of Adam before his fall." Every person, therefore, "is able to resist every sin [and] he must do so." In his larger work on the *History of Dogma,* 5:175, (quoted in Sproul, *Faith Alone,* 136), Harnack refers to the Pelagian doctrine as stated at the Synod of Carthage in the year 418 as claiming that "man can be without sin and keep the divine commands easily if he will." For Pelagianism in its varying degrees the will is perfectly free to accept or reject the offer of salvation that Christ provided. Effectively, therefore, anyone who is saved is saved by his own decision and choice, and the sovereign grace of God is not necessarily involved in salvation in any prior sense. Man effectively saves himself. That is "autosoterism." In the semi-Pelagianism of Roman Catholic theology, salvation is a matter of cooperation between the grace of God and the freewill choice of the individual person. That is effectively a "synergism." It again diminishes the biblical meaning of the grace of God and robs God of his sovereignty. Salvation, as we shall go on to see, is a "divine monergism" (salvation is due to God alone), not an "autosoterism" or a divine-human "synergism."

of the administration of God's covenant of grace. We speak, therefore, of covenantal justification.

We have referred to the fact that salvation is a divine monergism because it is grounded in the divinely-appointed and substitutionary suffering, obedience, sacrifice, resurrection, and heavenly session of Christ. That monergism is further exhibited in the fact that the individual's saving faith, the instrumental cause of justification, is in turn the sovereign and unsolicited endowment of the Spirit of God to the human soul. We say, therefore, that the suffering of Christ is to be understood as a covenantal suffering, as his incarnation was a covenantal incarnation, his obedience and death a covenantal obedience and death, and all of the aspects of his salvific accomplishment are in the same manner covenantally qualified. The monergistic circle that establishes and guarantees salvation is closed, accordingly, in the reality that saving faith is itself to be understood as covenantal faith. That is to say, all aspects of salvation occur within, and they discover their full meaning under the rubric of, the covenant of grace. For that reason, we conclude that what is customarily referred to as the elements of the *ordo salutis*, as well as the acts of God that are aspects of the accomplishment of redemption, are to be understood as covenantally qualified in the sense we have stated.

Covenant-making God

To see clearly what is at issue in the relations we have raised it is necessary to adduce briefly certain aspects of God's self-revelation and his revelatory statement of purpose. We acknowledge, first, that all of reality external to the Godhead is, by virtue of God's creative word, covenantally structured. By God's creative fiat, reality was structured in such a way as to conduce to the glory of God, and when the day of creation's groaning because of sin is ended the proclamation of God's glory will be complete, eternal, and everywhere visibly declared. The objectives of God's covenant with his creation, both his real and personal creation, will then be realized, a consummation guaranteed by reason of the cosmic significance of the work of Christ. But of immediate concern is that within that covenantal creation structure man himself is a covenant creature. We shall see some of the implications of that in the discussion of our first parents' repudiation of their covenantal obligations and the rescue that the covenant of grace has provided. For sin, we shall observe, is in its essence a repudiation of covenantal obligations.

The terms and significance of God's salvific covenant are to be seen as reflecting the self-disclosure that God has made. To understand God's salvific purpose, it is necessary to reflect, first, on what God has revealed as to his being and holiness. We hold at the beginning to the aseity of God, in that in his being and existence he is not dependent on any cause external to himself. If it were imagined that there was any entity, law, canon, or possibility external to the Godhead on which God was dependent or to which he stood eternally in relation, we would be speaking of a god lower than the eternal God who has revealed himself in the ways the Scriptures declare. When he spoke into existence all reality external to the Godhead, God created time as a mode of finite existence, and he spoke that reality into the time that he had made. In his eternal day he exists outside of time. His knowledge of himself and of external reality, therefore, is timeless. In his timelessness God knew all things in one eternal act of knowing. He does not wait to discover. His knowledge is not sequential. He neither remembers nor forgets, because he knows all things in that eternal moment. He therefore does not wait to discover his own future. He does not change, but in his eternal will he wills all changes. Because he has willed the future he knows the future and he does not wait to discover it or what it will contain. We bow before the mystery.

In making those statements we have firmly rejected the recent claims of Open Theism as a system of theology on which we commented in an earlier chapter. The claim of Open Theism that God cannot know the future contains the essence of the so-called "Process Theology" that was current in the twentieth century and which claims, as Paul Helm has summarized it, "not only that God is in time but that it is essential to God that he changes, that his own character matures as he experiences the love, disappointment, and frustration of his creation."[3]

Now it is not necessary to speak further at length at this time of the doctrine of God, or, that is, of theology proper. But to see the manner of accomplishment of his saving purpose we bring into focus on the basis of the scriptural data God's existence as a trinity of Persons, such that the full essence of the Godhead resides in each of the Persons. Given the eternal autotheotic (existing as God in his own right) nature of the Son and the Holy Spirit, both the Son and the Holy Spirit are fully God. An instance of what is involved is contained in the words of our Lord himself: "I and my Father are one" (John 10:30), and Christ referred to himself as "the Son of

---

3. Helm, *Eternal God*, xi.

man which is in heaven" (John 3:13). If, contrary to our doctrine that the full essence of God is the possession of each of the divine Persons, we were to say that the essence of God was distributed among the Persons, we would then be speaking of not a trinity, but of a quaternity of entities, namely the three divine Persons plus the essence that was in some sense shared between them. We would in that case be not trinitarians but quaternitarians.

As we wish to hold in view the redemptive offices of the Persons of the Godhead, we note from the statement we have just made the autotheotic nature of both the second and third Persons of the Godhead. Of God the Son we say that as to his nature he is autotheotic, while as to his Person he is of the Father. And of the Holy Spirit we say that as to his nature he is autotheotic, while as to his Person he is of the Father and the Son. In holding to that formulation, we are in agreement with the *filioque* clause in the Niceno-Constantinopolitan creed which, as we have it today, states that "the Holy Spirit . . . proceeds from the Father and the Son."[4]

We refer, now, to the divine council of redemption in which the three Persons of the Godhead were engaged. We have it at Ephesians 1:11 that God "worketh all things after the counsel of his own will." We bring to emphasis that the "coun*sel*" of God was the outcome of the divine "coun*cil*." We do so in order to hold in view at the same time the distinguishable hypostases (persons) of the Father, the Son, and the Holy Spirit, while we hold to the mysterious truth that the full essence of the Godhead resides in each of the Persons. We have referred in that connection to the perichoresis, or the mutual indwelling, of the Persons of the Godhead. We hold to the simplicity of God, meaning that God is not made up of parts. He is, as the *Westminster Confession* states, "without body, parts or passion."[5] We are directed, thereby, to consider the distinguishable redemptive offices assumed by the respective Persons of the Godhead in the accomplishment and application of redemption. What, then, is to be said of the outcome of the divine council?

---

4. The word *filioque* (and from the Son) was current at the time of the earlier councils of the church (Nicea, 325, Constantinople, 381, Ephesus, 431, and Chalcedon, 451), but the clause was inserted in the creed only at the Synod of Toledo in 589. Its incorporation in the creed gave rise to what was henceforth referred to as "the Filioque clause," and its adoption became the occasion of a divergence between the Western and Eastern churches that remains at the present time. The Eastern church continues to reject the filioque clause.

5. *Westminster Confession of Faith*, II:I. The "without passion" in that statement is saying that the essence of God, God in his eternal being, is not changed by the eventuation of any contingency in time.

God's covenantal declaration

We are interested at this point in two questions, having to do with both the *parties* to God's covenants on the one hand, and the *subjects* of the covenants on the other. As to the covenant of redemption, we have already implied that the parties to the covenantal agreement and undertaking were the three Persons of the Godhead in their distinguishable personhoods. The redemptive office of the Father was that of electing a designated people for redemption and his giving those persons to his Son to redeem. In his assumption of his redemptive office, the Son voluntarily undertook to come into the world, to assume human nature into union with his divine nature (yet without sin), to satisfy the demands of God's law on behalf of, and to bear in his death the penalty of the guilt of the sin of, those whom the Father had given to him for that purpose. The Holy Spirit undertook to apply to those people in due time the benefits of the redemption that Christ accomplished and to conduct them to glory.

In order to realize the objectives of the covenant of redemption thus declared, it was necessary, as has already been seen, to establish what we may refer to as an implementing covenant that is contemplated as the covenant of grace. The *parties* to the covenant of grace are God on the one hand, and those whom he has chosen to redeem on the other. Or more particularly, we may say that the parties were God on the one hand and the *subjects* of the covenant *as they were represented by Christ*. We leave aside for the present a not unimportant question that has exercised the mind of the church from time to time, namely that of whether we should take a supralapsarian (before the fall) or an infralapsarian (after the fall) view of the subjects of the covenant of grace.[6]

More important for the present is the fact that the subjects of the decree to redeem, the subjects who were the beneficiaries of the redemption that Christ provided, and the subjects of the Holy Spirit's undertaking to sanctify and conduct to glory were precisely the same persons. It is important to insist on that relation because it has been denied by errant doctrines of salvation such, for example, as that of the Arminians. For in that scheme of things it is argued that Christ died, in fact, for all men indiscriminately. But as to the calling and sanctifying work of the Holy Spirit, it is claimed that the subjects of the Spirit's work are not *all* men, but only *some* men. In

---

6. We observed in the preceding chapter that our argument implied an infralapsarian view of the covenant of grace. "Infralapsarian" means that the subjects of the decree to redeem were fallen people.

the Arminian scheme, the Holy Spirit conducts his work of applying the benefits of the death of Christ only to those who, in their sovereign decision, accept the offer of salvation that Christ provided.

The first and successive statements of the gospel

It was seen in a previous chapter, where the summary statements of the apostle John were adduced, that the first statement of the gospel is not a statement about man, sin, or even the work of Christ, but is a statement about God. God, John states at the beginning of his first epistle, is a holy God. "God is light and in him is no darkness at all" (1 John 1:5). It is true, of course, that the gospel is addressed to fallen and sinful men (using the word "men" at this point generically to refer to all people). But though it is addressed to men, the first statement it makes is not about men. It is not directly about the condition in which men stand as the gospel comes to them. The first statement of the gospel, which, clearly, should determine the form of the declaration of it, is a statement about God. It is the statement that we have to do with a holy God, and then it will follow in the second place that the only real and true explanation of the human condition turns on the fact that the state of sin in which we stand as a result of Adam's fall is that we have offended and outraged the holiness of God.

At that point, then, we can legitimately announce the further words of the gospel. The gospel, that is, is at a minimum, and apart from the wider aspects and implications of it, a three-part statement. We can go so far as to say that it is a reliable criterion of proper preaching to consider the relation that exists between those parts. The first statement is, as we have seen, that we have to do with a holy God. The second statement has to do with the explanation of the state in which we stand as the gospel comes to us. And the third statement is that which clarifies the substitutionary work of Christ by which sinners are redeemed. The second and third parts of that declaration of the gospel as the apostles contemplated them are clear: Christ died for sinners (1 Tim 1:15) and in due time Christ died for the ungodly (Rom 5:6).

The statement of the confession that we adduced at the beginning now comes into clearer focus. The sinner's critical need, it is rightly said, is the discovery of some means to attain to "justification, sanctification, and eternal life." The instrumental condition the gospel announces at that point is the repentant sinner's "accepting, receiving, and resting on Christ alone." But the twofold question arises as to why, more precisely, that condition is what it is, and what it is about the work of Christ that makes the fulfillment of the conditions effective to the desired end. We take the first of those questions first. In doing so, we discover a direct linkage to the terms of the covenant of grace that the confession has already invoked in the same context.

The gospel comes to those whose natural state of alienation from God is what it is because of their inheritance of the guilt of Adam's sin. Adam had been established by God as a public person, in the sense that he was the federal or representative head of all those who were to descend from him by ordinary generation. By reason of the immediate imputation to them of the guilt of Adam's sin they were constituted sinners. And as a result, all individuals come into the world with a fallen and sinful nature. We keep clear in our doctrine the twofold implication for Adam's posterity of his dereliction from the obligations of the covenant in which God had established him: first, the imputation to his posterity of the guilt of Adam's sin; and second, the transmission of a fallen nature with which all men come into the world. But in the interest of doctrinal precision it is not true to say that all men are sinners because they come into the world with a fallen nature. The contrary is true. All men come into the world with a fallen nature because they were constituted sinners by Adam's fall. The fifth chapter of the letter to the Romans is eloquent on the point (Rom 5:12-21). The question to be addressed is not why God should have ordained that the consequences of Adam's sin should involve his posterity in the respect stated. The fact is that God in the wisdom of his will and intention ordered and structured his creation in that manner. Mystery exists in God's action in involving all men in Adam's sinful act. John Murray judiciously observes that "it is not ours to solve all mysteries and by no means ours to call in question the government of God in inflicting the whole race with the penal consequences of Adam's own sin."[7] We observe that because God spoke all things, real and personal, into existence, they remain his property, and he is free to do with them what he wills. It is clear from the word that God has given in the Scriptures that his ordinations and intentions with regard to all men are informed by his grace and love. It was the love of God that sent his Son to be the propitiation for our sin (1 John 4:10).

But what, we must ask, was the primeval sin that spread its infection to Adam's race? The terms of the probation under which our first parents were established are well known. In the event, they ate of the forbidden

---

7. Murray, *Imputation*, 85.

fruit. But in construing the meaning of their sin it is appropriate to recall that they were created as covenant creatures. God at the beginning, we have said, spoke all things external to the Godhead into existence. The all things included all real and material things and our first parents who were created in his image. In that speaking into existence, all of reality, including, as we are now observing it, the human situation, was covenantally structured. As to our first parents, it is not that God created Adam and Eve and then superimposed his image on them, so that they became his image bearers. Rather, in his very constitution man *is* the image of God. He is the image of God in that he is created a rational, immortal, spiritual, moral, and speaking person.[8] And notwithstanding his inheritance of the effects of Adam's fall he remains the image of God. Man in sin is still a rational, immortal, spiritual, moral, and speaking person. It is that that underlies his continuing obligation to God from whose hands he has come.

That man is a covenant creature requires us to hold in view that at his creation he sustained, or was liable to, certain covenantal obligations. Those obligations included the mandate to discharge to the glory of God the offices of prophet, priest, and king. Adam was to be a prophet in that he was to investigate, understand, and explain the meaning of the reality in which he had come to self-consciousness. His office as priest required him to dedicate that knowledge and understanding back to God, to live continuously in the state of holiness in which he stood, and to construct his life as a worship of God. He was to rule as a king over all of reality to the glory of God. But the meaning of his fall, in one of its most significant implications, is that as a result, he was no longer able to discharge those prophetic, priestly, and kingly offices and obligations.

In essence, Adam was obligated under the terms of the covenant of creation, sometimes referred to as the covenant of works under which he stood in relation to God, to conduct his life in obedience to the law of God. Obedience to law is of the essence of covenantal obligation. It is for that reason that the apostle summarized the relations involved in, first, the sin of Adam, and second, the rescue provided by Christ in precisely those terms. "For as by one man's *disobedience* many were made sinners, so by the *obedience* of one shall many be made righteous" (Rom 5:19). The knowledge of the law of God was inherent in Adam's created constitution, because for Adam to *be* was to *know*. In his pristine holy state he naturally knew God,

---

8. I have discussed man as the image of God more fully in my *Christian Confession*, chapter 3.

he knew he had come from the hands of God, and he naturally knew and initially loved the law of God. The harmony of the faculties of soul that characterized his finite humanity was such that he was, at his creation, constitutionally holy.

The essence of Adam's sin is that in it he repudiated his covenantal obligations. That is always and essentially at its root the meaning of sin. Sin in its essence, we have said, is the denial and repudiation of covenantal obligations. Adam was created in a state of constitutive holiness and righteousness. He was holy in that in all his faculties he was aligned to obedience to the law of God. He was righteous in that all of his decisions and actions prior to his fall were consistent with, and were informed by, the holiness of the state in which he stood. But in his finitude he was defectible, mutable, in a state of *posse non peccare* (possible not to sin) but, as became too well-known, it was possible for him to fall. The denial of his covenantal obligation to live under the law of God came to expression in his assertion of autonomy from God. That assertion of autonomy, false and disastrous as it was, is most sharply instanced by his misuse of the rational faculty that had, up to that time, guided and determined all of his actions of soul. For when the tempter presented him with the lie that seduced him, he found himself in a strangely new position. Here he was confronted with two possible lines of action. He was now confronted with a mandate from his Creator and with a contrary suggestion and invitation from the devil. Which should he then choose? In effect Adam decided he would not automatically and with reflex action choose or believe either one or the other. Rather, and in this his assertion of autonomy enters, he would make up his own mind what he should choose and do.[9] In that assertion of autonomy it became only too clear that he had, in fact, sold his soul to the devil. As that is the origin of sin, it has remained ever since the essential nature of sin, the false assertion of human autonomy against God.

We may now summarize in covenantal terms the meaning of what has been said. For the initial and created covenantal status that our first parents enjoyed projects its implications for all men since. Adam's created relationship to God and the obligations of obedience to the mandates of God that he thereby sustained are construed under what is referred to as a covenant of works. When Adam sinned, the obligations to which he and all of his posterity were liable under the covenant of works were in no sense

---

9. The argument that has just been made has been explored more fully by Van Til in his *Theory of Knowledge*, 41–71. See also Frame, *History*, 54.

abolished. All men since remain obligated to fulfill the requirements of the covenant of works in order that God will be honored as his holiness demands and requires.[10] If Adam had sustained his probation he would have been confirmed in holy state and admitted to eternal life. It is true that some theologians demur from the suggestion that if Adam had remained obedient to his covenantal obligations he would have *merited* eternal life. The notion of merit at that point is rejected by certain theological constructions. But we can hold with many Reformed theologians that as Charles Hodge, for example, has commented, "Had he [Adam] retained his integrity he would have *merited* the promised blessing."[11] That Adam would have merited the blessing of eternal confirmation in holy state as a reward for his obedience is clear from the fact that the second Adam, Christ, merited *his* reward on the grounds of *his* obedience. For the first Adam was a type of the second.

When we say that the obligations of the covenant of works remain for all men we are not saying that the covenant of works remains a way of life. While the covenant of works does not now continue as a way of entrance to life as it did in Adam's initial state, the sinner in his natural state remains exposed to the curse that the covenant contemplated in the event of disobedience. A. A. Hodge, son of Charles Hodge and his successor at Princeton Theological Seminary in the nineteenth century, has commented that "This Covenant having been broken by Adam . . . and Christ having fulfilled all of its conditions in behalf of all his people . . . the covenant of works having been fulfilled by the second Adam is henceforth abrogated under the gospel. Nevertheless, since it is founded upon the principles of immutable justice, *it still binds all men who have not fled to the refuge offered in the righteousness of Christ.*"[12]

Hodge's statement introduces us to the third element of the gospel. What, then, has Christ done in order that sinners might be redeemed and might be reestablished in reconciliation with God? We may put the answer in a sentence. The Second Person of the Godhead came into the world to become Jesus Christ for our redemption and to do for us what we were obligated to do under the covenant of works but were unable to do for

---

10. For a more expansive discussion of the prelapsarian covenant, see Vickers, *Divine Redemption*, chapters 2 and 3, noting also comments there on certain attempts in contemporary theology to diminish and disregard the continued relevance of the covenant of works.

11. Hodge, C. *Systematic Theology* 2:364, italics added.

12. Hodge, A. A. *Outlines of Theology*, 314, italics added.

ourselves; in doing that, he fulfilled the previously unfulfilled obligations under the covenant of works for which we were liable, but which we could not fulfill by reason of the state of sin in which we were bound. The relationship involved can therefore be put by observing that the covenant of grace was established, with the parties to it, the subjects it contemplated, and the requirements and objectives it specified, in order to provide a remedy for the delinquency under the covenant of works for which the people of God were liable.

Why, then, does the confessional statement with which we began state that "accepting, receiving, and resting upon Christ alone" is the way to the realization of the benefits of "justification, sanctification, and eternal life?" It is because, as the hymn writer Cecil Frances Alexander captured the meaning of it: "There was no other good enough to pay the price of sin; / he only could unlock the gate of heav'n, and let us in."[13] If we can speak with extreme care and with humility, it could be said that the problem that faced the Godhead in eternity was that of how any from among the offspring of Adam could be rescued from the state of sin to which they had fallen. As we have seen, the mystery of redemption is that a distribution of redemptive offices among the Persons of the Godhead meant that the Second Person, God the Son, would come into the world to redeem a people in the manner we have observed.

Because sin had entered the world in human nature it was necessary that the penalty for sin should be paid in human nature. The remarkable thing to be said regarding the accomplishment of redemption is that God himself gave for our sin what it was his own justice demanded. The Second Person of the Godhead came, therefore, to be our redeemer. He came as the great high priest, the antitype of the earlier Levitical priests, to administer the definitive sacrifice for sin and to be himself the offering that satisfied divine justice. He was not always Jesus Christ. He came into the world in order to *become* Jesus Christ. He came to die *in his human nature*, that the entailment of sin as it devolved on the people of God might be broken and that they might again be reconciled to him.[14]

It is within the divinely-assured covenantal purpose of God that those whom God the Father, in the distribution of redemptive offices located in

---

13. Alexander, "There Is a Green Hill Far Away," In *Trinity Hymnal*, 256.

14. I leave aside at this point the extensive discussion in the literature regarding what have been referred to as differing theories of the atonement. See Vickers, *Divine Redemption*, 17–22, for a discussion of the early statement of the satisfaction theory of the atonement by Anselm, who served as Archbishop of Canterbury, 1093–1109.

divine council, gave to his Son to redeem will in fact be drawn to him in the Spirit-endowed gifts of saving faith and repentance. "All that the Father giveth me" our Lord said, "shall come to me, and him that cometh to me I will in no wise cast out" (John 6:37). And in the same context he said that "No man can come to me except the Father which hath sent me draw him" (John 6:44). Our Lord at that point was speaking in terms that he had spoken through the prophet Jeremiah of old: "I have loved thee with an everlasting love; therefore with lovingkindness have I drawn thee" (Jer 31:3).

The elements of saving faith are clear in the confessional statement with which we began: "accepting, receiving, and resting on Christ alone." For those who come to Christ in saving faith and repentance the benefits of the covenantal promise are immediately assured.

The *Westminster Shorter Catechism* sums up the issue. "Justification is an act of God's free grace, wherein he pardoneth all our sins, and accepteth us as righteous in his sight, only for the righteousness of Christ, imputed to us, and received by faith alone."[15] "Repentance unto life is a saving grace, whereby a sinner, out of a true sense of his sin, and apprehension of the mercy of God in Christ, doth, with grief and hatred of his sin, turn from it unto God, with full purpose of, and endeavor after, new obedience."[16]

The issue is resolved in the words of the Confession. Those who come in trust and saving faith in Christ will know the joys of freedom from the guilt of sin, the calmness of soul that rest in him provides, and the assurance, as the Confession of Faith states it, of eternal life.

---

15. *Westminster Shorter Catechism*, Question 33.
16. Ibid., Question 87.

Chapter 6

The Covenantal Christian Life

THE STATEMENT OF THE Confession that has motivated our study, as it was referred to at the beginning of the preceding chapter, has important implications for the on-going Christian life. The very acts that conduce to the objectives of justification, sanctification, and eternal life, the *means* as well as the *objectives* and *ends*, have been ordained as integral to the divine formation of the covenant of grace. That is what we mean by saying that all of the parts and aspects of our redemption to eternal life are what they are by the grace of God. Let us now look at some aspects of what is involved in that respect.

First, with recognition again of the pervasive implications of the fact that God's relations with his people are covenantal relations, God's covenantal lordship comes to effect in that he "works all things according to the counsel of his own will" (Eph 1:11). If, as we have said, God in that divine working is sovereign in and over all of the affairs of men, does that sovereignty extend, we may ask, to *all* of the *actions* of men? We answer in the affirmative. Further, does that sovereignty extend to all of the *thoughts* of men? We again answer in the affirmative. And in that answer, as we shall see, we are anticipating a highly significant aspect of the work of the Holy Spirit in the process of the Christian believer's sanctification. In other words, the all-comprehending sovereignty of God requires it to be said that it is not possible for any individual to *do* anything that God has not ordained. It is not possible for man to *do* anything that God has not already thought. But further, our claim is that it is not possible for any individual to *think* anything that God has not already thought. "I know the thoughts that come into your mind," God has said, "every one of them" (Ezek 11:5).

He knows the thought because he ordained the thought. "The lot is cast into the lap; but the whole disposing thereof is of the Lord" (Prov 16:33). More particularly, "The king's heart is in the hand of the Lord, as the rivers of water; he turneth it whithersoever he will" (Prov 21:1).

The meaning of what is involved might be startling on its surface and it no doubt challenges in our thought the question of individual personal freedom or, as it most forcibly comes to expression, the freedom of the human will. But it would be grossly inadequate to say that the Spirit of God orders only the *external* events and experiences in the life of the individual he is committed to bring to glory. The Spirit moves in the *innermost recesses of the soul*. He thinks the thoughts of holiness in us, and he thereby structures our lives and our progress. What else would be the meaning and import of the apostle's exclamation to the Galatians, "I live; yet not I, but Christ liveth in me" (Gal 2:20)? The hymn writer, Harriet Auber, has captured the meaning of what is involved in the hymn that begins, "Our blest Redeemer, ere He breathed / His tender, last farewell, / A guide, a comforter, bequeathed / With us to dwell." And in the penultimate stanza of the hymn the writer reflects on the ministry of that Comforter to the soul and states significantly that "Every thought of holiness [is] his alone."[1]

Secondly, we acknowledge that there is a mystery involved in the sovereign work of the Spirit of God in the soul of man. That mystery exists within the orbit of the working of the Spirit at the same time as the individual person himself works out his salvation. "Work out your own salvation with fear and trembling. For it is God which worketh in you both to will and to do of his good pleasure" (Phil 2:12-13). The statement is not simply to the effect that God by his grace gives to his people the ability and power to live in obedience to him. For the law of God remains the rule of life for God's people. That God does give grace to his people to that effect is, of course, true. But the text from the Philippian letter is saying, beyond that, that God does in fact accomplish in the lives of his people what he has ordained as the parts and progress of their conformation in holiness to the image of his Son. The Spirit is sovereign in sanctification. In that sovereignty he is working sanctification in his people by communicating to them the communicable attributes of God to the extent that, and in the degree that, he is preparing them for the place God has ordained they will occupy in the eternal kingdom of glory. The work of the Holy Spirit in preparing the saints of God for their place in glory is analogous to what was involved

---

1. Auber, *Our blest Redeemer*, 209.

in the preparation for the temple that Solomon built. "The house, when it was building, was built of stone made ready before it was brought thither; so that there was neither hammer nor axe nor any tool of iron heard in the house, while it was building" (1 Kings 6:7). In a corresponding manner, the Holy Spirit is at work in this life preparing his people for their place in heaven. For at the point of entrance to heaven the preparation will have been completed. There will be no further sanctification in heaven. The preparatory process of sanctification will have come to an end, and all will be ready for the glorious eternal temple of God. In the process to that end, the Spirit so supervises, orders, directs, and guides the operation of personal free wills that all that he has purposed does in fact eventuate.

But there is a further point to be noted. When the apostle states that God works in the Christian person "to will and to do of his good pleasure," a further and deeper divine prospect and objective come into view. The burden of the text should not be restricted to a manward aspect of what is involved, in the sense that concentration is confined to the benefits that accrue to the individual Christian in his own right. What the text contemplates is to be understood as contributing to the individual person's sanctification in the manner we have just observed. But in all of the divine working in and with his people, God's larger covenantal purposes and objectives must be held in view. What is involved in the Philippians statement, then, is that God has bestowed on the Christian believer, and that he continues by his sanctifying grace to bestow on his people, the high privilege of their being, under God, the means of furthering the realization of what God has purposed to do "of his good pleasure."

That is so in the sense, again, that it reflects what is to be said regarding God's purpose that all things should be done to his glory and should reflect his glory. God's glory consists in the demonstration to all his rational creatures, in heaven and in earth, of his infinite perfections. And when the Christian is enjoined to do all things to the glory of God (1 Cor 10:31), he is given the high privilege of being the reflection of that glory, in being the vehicle in whatever way God ordains of participating in and contributing to that high objective. So it is in the present case of the Christian believer's progress in sanctification. God works in the lives of his people in such a way that a twofold objective will be realized. First, by his working in them he gives them the motivation and encouragement to persevere in their part in the process of their sanctification. And second, by doing so he is using his sanctified people to further his objective of demonstrating his own glory. That is the high privilege of the Christian life.

But what is to be said of individual freedom? An answer to the question is necessary in order to understand further the sovereignty of the Spirit in the Christian believer's sanctification and in, therefore, the subjection of sanctification to the terms of the covenant of grace.

We do not need to enter at this point the long and philosophic discussion of the freedom of the will. I have addressed that in other places.[2] The upshot of the question for our present purposes is that the individual will is not free in an isolated sense to determine its own action, but that it necessarily acts in conformity with the state, decisions, and motivations of the faculties of the soul. In Adam's prelapsarian state there existed an undisturbed harmony among the faculties. The soul was then characterized by free will in the fullest sense. The *Westminster Shorter Catechism* makes the point. When our first parents were "left to the *freedom of their own will*" they "fell from the estate wherein they were created."[3] That initial state of free will existed because the mind, the intellectual faculty, naturally knew God and responded with clarity and uncluttered reason to the knowledge of God that was inherent in Adam's created condition. At the same time, with the affective or emotional faculty Adam naturally loved God, and the natural disposition, the *habitus* implicit in the soul, moved our first parent to love the law of God and to love the work of obedience to it. In harmonious concurrence, then, the will was naturally instructed to obey God. There was at that time no discordance or possibility of disruption among the faculties so long as the initial state of righteousness was preserved.[4]

A highly significant sense exists, therefore, in which it can be said that at the fall man lost his free will. His intellectual faculty was henceforth blinded by the god of this world (2 Cor 4:4; 1 Cor 2:14) and his emotional faculty was enslaved by the devil to the extent that he was now a God-hater (Rom 1:30). Because with the mind man could no longer *know* God and the good that he required, and because with the heart now turned from God and enslaved to sin he could not *love* the good, the mind and the heart could no longer instruct the will to *do* the good. That was the sorry state to which Adam and his posterity were reduced by his dereliction from what

---

2. See Vickers, *Immediacy of God*, chapters 3–5.

3. *Westminster Shorter Catechism*, Question 13, italics added.

4. See the discussion in Cunningham, on "The Doctrine of the Will," in *Historical Theology*, I:568–639.

God's covenant had required of him. We have seen that as a result of the fall man is disabled from the initial functions and prerogatives with which he was created. But as to action in general, and apart from the precise question of the knowledge of God and actions in accordance with the mandates of God, the question persists whether there exists any respect in which the will can be said to be free.

Our response must be that in all respects, and by the very nature of the constitution of the soul and human personhood, the will remains under the inevitable influence of the intellectual and emotional deliberations. When Jonathan Edwards said that the action of the will is "as the greatest apparent good is,"[5] he was laying down a principle which, of necessity, is universally explanatory of willing action. For example, a man may well have decided at one time or another that excessive consumption of alcohol is a thing which, on the basis of his own established moral principles, he will avoid. But if, on a certain occasion, he takes alcohol to an excess and thereby defies what he had previously laid down as a moral principle, it is not to be said that he is doing so against his will. Nor can it properly be said that his will is free, in an isolated and independent sense, to take the alcohol or not take it. The situation in strict reality is that he took the alcohol because, at the point of taking it, it was apparent to him that in the situation that then existed that action was seen as "his greatest apparent good." His reason and his emotional preferences at that time dictated that the preponderance of good rested in the action he then took. The action of taking the alcohol was not an independent act of the will. It was an act of the whole person.

What has just been said finds precise application in the ministry of the Spirit of God to and in the Christian life. While the will is free from outside compulsion, and while an individual cannot be forced to do something he does not will to do, nevertheless it is necessarily subject to the internal faculties of the soul in the manner we have seen, and, it can now be said, is subject to the mysterious supervision and direction of the will of God. For in the will of God, and under the control of the sovereign ordering of God, all of the forces of history and the formation of character that bear on the formation and functioning of an individual's faculties transmit their effects, impulses, and determinations to the will and its actions.

The significance of what has been said for the individual believer's progress in sanctification is clear. God works, and man works. But that working of God and man does not amount to a synergism such as is to

---

5. Edwards, *Freedom of the Will*, 86.

be rejected when we speak of man's justification and reconciliation with God. In that case there is not, and there could not be, any possibility of synergism, because at the time of the coming of the renewing grace of God the individual is "dead in trespasses and sins" (Eph 2:1). In the present case of progress in sanctification, the working of the Christian person in the discharge of his ethical responsibilities that point to his sanctification is, as has now been said, decidedly under the supervision, direction, and support of the Holy Spirit.

We reflect further on what we have already contemplated as the divine covenant of redemption, and we recall the distribution of redemptive offices among the triune Persons, the Father, the Son, and the Holy Spirit. It was the declared and assigned office of the Holy Spirit to apply to those for whom Christ died the benefits of the redemption he accomplished and to conduct them to glory. But Paul has stated to the Corinthians that it is Christ who is the Christian's sanctification. Christ is "of God made unto us wisdom, and righteousness, and *sanctification*, and redemption" (1 Cor 1:30, italics added). That attribution to Christ is necessary and meaningful in two respects. First, it is the completion of the messianic-redemptive work of Christ that forms the basis of, or that provides the divinely accepted warrant for, the Holy Spirit's work of sanctification. Second, when the relation between the work of Christ and that of the Spirit is seen in the form in which Christ himself stated it, it is clear that it is Christ himself who is accomplishing the Christian's sanctifiction through his Spirit. For in his discourse to his disciples on the night on which he was betrayed he had given them the promise and explanation that "when he, the Spirit of truth, is come, he will guide you into all truth: for he shall not speak of himself; but whatsoever he shall hear, that shall he speak... He shall glorify me: for he shall receive of mine, and show it unto you" (John 16:13-14).

Eternal life

Finally, we note from the confessional statement that has motivated our discussion that by virtue of the covenant of grace we have not only justification and sanctification, but, with that, eternal life. In the light of all we have said to this point some concluding observations can be made. Essentially, two questions are involved. First, it is necessary to see the interdependence between those threefold benefits of redemption and to appreciate their joint and several relations to God's announced terms of the covenant. And second, it is necessary, in the light of certain questionable proposals that have been made for paradigm changes in Reformed theology, to be clear as to what God's covenantal statement of justification does *not* mean and imply.

A careful reading of the Confession makes it clear that "eternal life," as it is there stated as the culminating blessing of the covenant, is to be seen as referring to the state in which the Christian believer is established as a result of what God had ordained as the requirements of the covenant of grace. But eternal life, as the Confession brings that into focus at that point, is not to be understood as a blessing that is *conditional upon*, in the sense that it *awaits*, justification and sanctification. It is true that a full realization of the fact and the benefits of eternal life *follows experientially* those other blessings. But the entrance to eternal life is to be guarded as *prior* to justification. That is because the entrance to eternal life turns on the fact, and the Holy Spirit's act, of an individual's regeneration by the sovereign grace of God. Regeneration is a sovereign, secret, and unsolicited act of the Holy Spirit whereby new life is created within the soul, the faculties of the soul are endowed with abilities and capacities they did not previously possess, and a new *habitus* or disposition or principle of action that seeks after God is implanted in the soul. It is appropriate to say that at regeneration the individual who is the beneficiary of that grace is "baptized into the body of Christ" (1 Cor 12:13), has the seal of God as belonging to him placed upon him, "sealed with that holy Spirit of promise" (Eph 1:13), and is joined to Christ in a vital and indissoluble union. The priority of that union has been well stated by Berkhof: "The initial act is that of Christ, who unites believers to himself *by regenerating them* and thus producing faith in them. On the other hand, the believer also unites himself to Christ by a conscious act of faith, and continues the union, under the influence of the Holy Spirit, by the constant exercise of faith."[6]

Berkhof has stated there concisely what we hold as the *ordo salutis*, or the order of application of redemption. He has emphasized the distinction between the *endowment* of faith on the one hand, or the endowment of the capacity to exercise faith, and the subsequent *exercise* of faith on the other. The *endowment* of faith is the *immediate* work of the Spirit of God that occurs at a point in time. The *exercise* of faith, or the activation of the newly endowed capacity of faith, occurs in time and may be characterized by any of several time dimensions. Murray observes in relation to those actions

---

6. Berkhof, *Systematic Theology*, 450, italics added.

that "regeneration pushes itself into consciousness and expresses itself in the exercises of faith and repentance."[7] But as to regeneration itself and the implications of it, Murray refers to regeneration as that act "of which faith and repentance are the immediate effects in our consciousness."[8]

God's statement of justification, consequent on the sinner's expression of faith and repentance, is, then, a once-for-all forensic statement that regards the sinner as "just" because the righteousness of Christ has been imputed to him, or placed to his account. In the most straightforward of terms, to be "just" in the eyes of God means that one's relation to the law of God is what it ought to be. It is precisely the absence of that "justness" that characterizes the state of sin. The declaration of the gospel, therefore, is that God himself establishes the necessary state by placing to the sinner's account the righteousness of Christ. We confront again the fact that Christ came into the world to be the sinner's substitute in the twofold aspect of keeping the law of God perfectly on the sinner's behalf and in paying the penalty of sin to which we were all exposed. We distinguish, then, between the *ground* on which God's statement of justification can be made on the one hand, and the *act* of justification on the other. The *ground* of justification is the completed substitutionary work of Christ. The *act* of justification follows God's response in time to the individual's exercise of faith and trust in Christ. It is true, of course, that there are aspects of the believer's realization of his eternal state that necessarily follow justification and sanctification. For the reality of eternal life expands its meaning to the state that will exist and be experienced in the life that is to come. But when, and because, the conditions necessary to justification and sanctification have been met (the work of Christ has fulfilled the conditions specified in the covenant of grace and the regenerating grace of God has conveyed the gift of faith to the soul) then at that point and at that time the believer is an indefectible partaker of eternal life.

But now that we have brought to further focus what is involved in justification and its relation to the state of sanctification, an important aspect of the divine action in justification should be observed. It is clearly stated in the Scriptures that "Christ died for the ungodly" (Rom 5:6), and that in doing so he bore the penalty of the guilt of those for whom he died (2 Cor 5:21). But the question arises: How could God the Father, in all justice, and remaining true to his eternal righteousness, punish in Christ

---

7. Murray, *Collected Writings*, 2:198.
8. Ibid., 115, italics added.

the sins of others when the penalty must properly be borne only by those who were guilty? God who is himself truthful and eternally righteous could not lay the punishment for sin on his Son unless his Son was actually guilty. What, then, was to be done? In order to be able truthfully to *declare* his Son guilty and therefore liable to punishment, and for God to remain true to his own righteousness, it was necessary that God should first *constitute* his Son guilty. That is precisely what was done. God *constituted* Christ guilty by imputing to him the guilt of those for whom he was about to die. Christ was not constituted a sinner. He was constituted guilty of sin, not of any sin of his own, for he was sinless, but guilty by transference to him of the sin of the people for whom he died. Because he had been constituted guilty, God could rightly and justly lay the punishment of sin on him. By the same token, God could not truthfully *declare* any persons to be righteous who were not, in fact, righteous. The truthfulness of God again intervened in the transaction. In order, therefore, to be able truthfully to *declare* certain individuals righteous, it was necessary that God should first *constitute* them as righteous. Again, that is precisely what was done. God *constituted* those people righteous by imputing to them the forensic righteousness of Christ. By that reciprocal transaction the justice of God remained unimpaired. God was therefore "Just, and the justifier of him which believeth in Jesus" (Rom 3:26).

On this highly important matter of constitutive righteousness, Murray has written insightfully: "Justification is both a declarative and a constitutive act of God's free grace. It is constitutive in order that it may be truly declarative. God must constitute the relationship as well as declare it to be. The constitutive act consists in the imputation to us of the obedience and righteousness of Christ."[9] Acknowledging that the truthfulness and righteousness of God are involved at that point, Turretin has stated in that connection: "God cannot show favor to, nor justify anyone without a perfect righteousness. For since the judgment of God is according to truth, he cannot pronounce anyone just who is not really just... By the righteousness and obedience of one, Christ, we are constituted righteous... Justification takes place on account of the suretyship of Christ and the payment made for us by him."[10]

When the purely forensic nature and meaning of justification are thus exposed, it is to be observed that God's action of justification does

---

9. See Murray, *Redemption*, 154. See also Murray, *Romans* I:203–206.
10. Turretin, *Institutes*, 2:647, 651, 653.

not make a person holy. Holiness is not involved at that point. But if it is not justification that makes a person holy, what does? The answer turns on the reality and meaning of God's conveyance to the sinner of the sovereign grace of regeneration. It is by regeneration that one is made holy, and that grace having done its work in the soul of an individual, he turns to Christ in saving faith in the manner we have seen. There is then an important sense in which holiness is prior to justification. By that we mean that a person is holy in the sense in which, having been the beneficiary of a new creating work of the Holy Spirit, he is set apart for God in a completely new relationship. By the secret work of the Spirit of God in regeneration, by being "born again," as Christ referred to it in his nocturnal conversation with Nicodemus (John 3:3), a sinner is thereby "delivered from the power of darkness, and translated into the kingdom of [God's] dear Son" (See Col 1:13). That work of regeneration constitutes the individual as holy, not only in the positional sense that he is now set apart for God, but in the sense also that the Holy Spirit's work of sanctification in the life of the individual has thereby begun. That is because the faculties of soul have been endowed with new abilities and capacities in the manner we have seen, and a new *habitus* or disposition or principle of action has been divinely implanted in the soul. What comes into view, as a result, is that, first, by regeneration one is made holy and his sanctification has begun; and secondly, by justification his status in relation to the law of God is radically changed to what it ought to be. In holiness and righteousness, then, the newborn person freely sets out on a life that is pleasing to God. Now and henceforth the Holy Spirit will so work in the life of the individual as to further his growth in holiness, or, as we shall see, his progressive sanctification.

Justification and sanctification, then, both involve declarative statements of God. We have already noted the once-for-all forensic statement of God that amounts to the repentant sinner's justification. Against that declarative statement, the sinner enters into a new experiential state, the state of *being* justified. "Therefore being justified ['having been justified'] by faith, we have peace with God" (Rom 5:1). We should see also that it is at the point of regeneration that the individual to whom that grace is communicated is thereby definitively and once-for-all transferred from the kingdom of Satan to the kingdom of God. At that point his transference from wrath to grace definitively occurs. God has thereby "delivered us from the power of darkness, and translated us into the kingdom of his dear Son" (Col 1:13). There is a once-for-allness about God's statements of justification, adoption into his family, and transference from the one kingdom to the other. The point to be grasped is that at the moment of regeneration sanctification has begun. Because that is so, we agree with John Murray's statements regarding what he refers to at that point as "definitive sanctification."[11] The new state of holiness in which the beneficiary of grace now stands is what is referred to as the individual's definitive sanctification. He is now holy in the sight of God.

Beyond that divine statement of definitive sanctification, however, is the progressive work of the Spirit in the life of the believer that amounts to what we have observed as his *progressive* sanctification. The redemptive work of God comes to consummation in the life of the individual by his deliverance from the guilt, the power, and the pollution of sin. We have inspected the deliverance from guilt under the heading of the justifying act of God, in the reciprocal imputation of the sinner's guilt to Christ and the imputation of Christ's forensic righteousness to the sinner. But it remains to be said that sin, that is actions of sin and even a principle of sin that wars against the soul, clings to the individual throughout his life in this world. It is the office of the Holy Spirit, then, to bring his divine influence to bear on the consciousness and life of the individual in such a way that the power of sin is progressively destroyed and the soul is progressively cleansed from the pollution of sin. That work of God in the soul takes up what is referred to as progressive sanctification, to which definitive sanctification is the necessary antecedent.[12]

Two observations need to be made in relation to certain claims by contemporary theologians that run counter to what we have said. First, it is in no sense true to say that justification awaits a forensic decision of God at the last day when, at the resurrection, we stand in judgment. Given what we have seen as the once-for-allness of God's forensic declarative statements to the repentant sinner, the individual person enters thereby into a *state* of justification that cannot be reversed. In the day of glory that individual will be more sanctified, but not more justified. Second, we recall our claim, which can be well understood on the basis of scriptural data, that at regeneration the individual is joined to Christ. The doctrine of the believer's union with Christ has been the subject of dispute and of erroneous statements and

---

11. See Murray, "Definitive Sanctification." In *Collected Writings,* 2:277.
12. See Murray, "Progressive Sanctification." In *Collected Writings,* 2:294.

conclusions in the recent New Perspective on Paul and the Federal Vision theologies. I have addressed those issues in other places.[13]

But it is to be held, as we have already said, that our union with Christ is indissoluble. It is in that last-mentioned fact that the confessional statement with which we began reaches its high and triumphant conclusion. It is "by virtue of the covenant of grace" that we have "eternal life." For it is an irrefutable datum of the Scriptures that, as our Lord himself prayed on our behalf, "This is life eternal, that they might know thee the only true God, and Jesus Christ, whom thou hast sent" (John 17:3). And we know God because we have heard his voice speaking to us in the Scriptures and in our Spirit-awakened consciences. And we have cast our state at the feet of Christ who, we now know, died in our place that we might be reconciled to God. We praise God for his spoken and clear Word, and for the salvation he has provided in his Son for all those who believe.

A concluding observation

A concluding observation is in order. We have looked carefully at the doctrinal content and significance of the remarkable confessional statement with which we began. By reason of the covenant of grace, sinners are brought to a condition of "accepting, receiving, and resting on Christ alone for justification, sanctification, and eternal life." It may very well be that we face a temptation to rest with some satisfaction in what we have worked out on that important and necessary doctrinal level. The danger exists that we might take satisfaction in what becomes, then, a mere or sheer intellectualism, or a fascination with a Reformed doctrinal scholasticism. It would be a pity if we fell subject to such a temptation. For our interest in doctrine and exegesis must never become a merely theoretical or academic interest. The objectives we have in view are quite different, and they must be reckoned to be different.

Let us hold to two implications of all that we have said, without which we finally fail: first, let us see what a firm grasp of our doctrines implies for the daily and continuing life in Christ Jesus to which, by the grace of God, we have been admitted; and second, let us be sure that our preaching and teaching of the word of life as we have found it to be revealed to us finds genuine application, both evangelistic and pastoral, as we follow out the

---

13. See Vickers, *When God Converts a Sinner*, chapter 7, and Vickers, *Immediacy of God*, 141 for a response to some recent claims of Horton in his *Covenant and Salvation*.

high privileges and responsibilities to which we have been called. Let us understand what it is, in its full-orbed meaning, that God has given to us as the evangel, and let that be reflected faithfully in our evangelism. Only then, in a balanced and well-rounded view of our doctrines and of their meaning and implications, will we have begun to honor the truths of which, by the sovereign grace of God, we are now the firm possessors.

Chapter 7

The Sabbath Obligation

IF THE CHURCH AT this time is to be the custodian of the evangel entrusted to it, and if the corresponding ordinances and obligations are to be faithfully transmitted to its evangelism, it is necessary to consider its stance in relation to the Sabbath Day. A principal conclusion of the argument that follows is that the church at this time should examine carefully where it stands on the doctrine of the Sabbath, what is required of it in that respect by God's ordination, and to what extent it has or has not been responsive to the corresponding obligations that God's covenantal prescriptions have laid upon it.

In the contemporary age of cultural confusion, the church does not command a significant place in the complex of ideas or affairs. In an important sense, of course, that has always been the case. A review of ecclesiastical history is not necessary to establish the point. God's characterization of his people of old as a "holy nation" (Exod 19:6), and the apostolic ascription to the church of the same designation (1 Pet 2:9), mean that the church has always been, or it should always have understood itself to be, separate from the world. Christianity, and the church as the custodian of God's revelation, have not been, and in the nature of the case they could not be, understood by the world. The church, when it is aware of its true identity, and the world live and move on contrary existential trajectories. But in the course of history, even since the Reformation rescued the church from its dogmatic slumber, there has been some intermeddling of the world and the church. Perhaps at the present time the indictment to be entered against the church is that in its doctrinal formulation, in its worship practice, and in its hospitality to alien idioms, the world is too much in the church. That

The Sabbath Obligation

in itself betrays the enigma of our position. The church has become more than ever like the world, but the agencies of the world despise the church.

If we say in response to such an analysis that the fault lies within the church itself, two important issues relevant to our subject press for recognition. They have to do with the question of *identity*, on the one hand, and that of *authority* on the other. We shall return to their import more fully at the conclusion of this chapter, but at this point a preliminary comment can be made.

The problem of *identity* means that in all too many instances, and perhaps in the general case, the confessing Christian is unaware in his practicing life of who he really is. He has forgotten that he is the redeemed and adopted child of the most high God, that he is joined to God in Christ in a vital and indissoluble union, and that the life of Christ by his Spirit courses within him. But beyond that, the Christian is all too easily unaware that he is, by creation and redemption, the property of God, that he is therefore subject to the obligations of the covenant of life that God has established with him, and that God has graciously articulated those obligations in the inscripturated word that he has given.

The problem of *authority* means that the Christian too readily relapses in practice to the old mechanics of autonomy from which, above all, the grace of God has rescued him. In the ordinary life and conduct of affairs the questions of criteria of belief and conduct are indistinctly understood and addressed. In short, the challenge to be raised is simply: Has God spoken? Is what God has said authoritative? And to what extent, with the new naturalness of holy conduct that should characterize Christian action, does the confessing Christian take into account the imperatives of the moral legislation that God has provided? As to God and his word as authoritative, we are reminded of the Scottish historian of the Reformation, William Cunningham, who observed in that connection that "authority, in its strict and proper sense, does not admit of degrees."[1]

It is a rewarding exercise to trace the views on the Sabbath obligation that have been held historically by the church and its principal spokesmen. That has been most ably done by James Dennison in his *The Market Day of the Soul*[2] and does not call for extended repetition at this point. It is of interest to note, however, that the English Puritan Sabbatarianism that is Dennison's main concern developed against the argument of the Roman

---

1. Cunningham, *Reformers*, 7.
2. Dennison, *Market Day of the Soul*, 1–166.

Catholic Council of Trent's catechism that the mandates of the Lord's Day were grounded simply in the authority of the ecclesiastical hierarchy. It is implicit in that claim that, as Dennison observes, "The Sabbath commandment does not share the same moral and perpetual character as the other nine."[3] The point is made at this initial stage because at this time a heavy burden of proof rests on the church to demonstrate that in its conception of the proprieties of the moral law, parity exists between all of the Ten Commandments. That parity, there is abundant cause to fear, is all too frequently honored in the breach. The Puritanism commitment, of course, was essentially Sabbatarian, the roots of which trace unmistakably to Calvin's doctrine.

Calvin's position on the Sabbath has itself been the subject of varying interpretations, and it has frequently been referred to as anti-Sabbatarian. It is fair to say, however, that that is a misreading of Calvin. In his commentary on the Decalogue in the *Institutes* he states explicitly "three conditions in which . . . the keeping of this commandment [the fourth] consists."[4] Calvin's three points of Sabbath doctrine were, firstly, that the Sabbath was a day of "spiritual rest in which believers ought to lay aside their own works to allow God to work in them" [We note there that a specific purpose is added to the abstinence from work, namely "to allow God to work in them," and in order that there might be, as Calvin saw it, a spiritual rest from sin]; secondly, it was to be a day of worship, "to hear the law [and] to devote it particularly to meditation upon his [God's] works, and thus through this remembrance to be trained in piety"; and thirdly, it was to be a "day of rest for servants."[5] Calvin's position was anti-Sabbatarian only in the sense that he rejected the Jewish insistence on the *ceremonial significance* of the seventh day. He argued that it was necessary to "transcend Judaism . . . for we are not celebrating [the seventh day] as a ceremony with the most rigid [Jewish] scrupulousness."[6] Calvin wanted nothing to do with "the false prophets who in former centuries infected the people with a Jewish opinion," and with what he refers to as "crass and carnal Sabbatarian superstition."[7] In his references to the Old Testament prophets on the point Calvin comments that "The Lord complains that his Sabbaths have been polluted, violated,

---

3. Dennison, *Market Day of the Soul*, 4.
4. Calvin, *Institutes*, 395. See *Institutes*, II-VIII-28–34.
5. Ibid., 395.
6. Ibid., 399.
7. Ibid., 400.

The Sabbath Obligation

not kept, not hallowed."[8] In the same context Calvin states that the Sabbath commandment is a "foreshadowing of spiritual rest,"[9] a spiritualizing of the Sabbath as a foreshadowing of the heavenly rest. He had made the point explicitly at the beginning of his comment on the seventh day: "The Lord through the seventh day has sketched for his people the coming perfection of his Sabbath in the Last Day, to make them aspire to this perfection by unceasing meditation upon the Sabbath throughout life."[10]

It is of particular notice that on the matter of the choice of the weekly day of worship, Calvin saw the Sabbath day as chosen by the church "as a remedy to keep order in the church"[11] and to provide, as he repeatedly stated it, a necessary day of worship.[12] It is not necessary to rehearse at this point the respects in which commentators have seen some ambiguities in Calvin's doctrine of the Sabbath, a matter that has been treated at length by Richard Gaffin.[13] Gaffin concludes his analysis with the deduction from Calvin's text that "Christians cannot be condemned who may wish to set apart some other day [than that chosen by the church] as long as they keep in view the need for stated times of worship and meditation."[14] But while that may be so, Calvin's clear statement should be noted that the church being free to choose a particular day of the seven as the day of worship, its choosing the first day of the week as the weekly Sabbath "lies in the Lord's resurrection."[15] It is clear that the church's change of the weekly Sabbath from the seventh to the first day of the week both preserves the divine mandate of devoting one day in seven to the worship of God, and at the same time honors the memory of the day of our Lord's resurrection. That change,

---

8. Ibid., 395.
9. Ibid., 395.
10. Ibid., 396.
11. Ibid., 399.

12. It is of interest that in connection with Calvin's statement that the Sabbath day is chosen by the church for purposes of good order, the editor of the edition of the *Institutes* cited, John T. McNeill, has observed at that point that "It is clear that for Calvin the Christian Sunday is not, as in the *Westminster Confession* II:XXI:8, a simple continuation of the Jewish Sabbath "changed into the first day of the week," but a distinctively Christian institution adopted on the abrogation of the former one, as a means of church order and spiritual health," *Institutes*, 399, fn. 41.

13. Gaffin, *Calvin and the Sabbath*.
14. Ibid., 395.
15. Calvin, *Institutes*, 399.

moreover, has clear apostolic imprimatur in the reference to "the first day of the week" at 1 Corinthians 16:2.

We may add that Calvin's statement in the *Institutes* of the first of his three points of Sabbath doctrine, that the Sabbath was a day of "spiritual rest in which believers ought to lay aside their own works to allow God to work in them," effectively provides the basic starting point from which an evaluation of his doctrine is to be made. That, we suggest, is his determinative viewpoint. Moreover, in the same context Calvin observes, with respect to the observance of the Sabbath as a day of rest for the purposes indicated, that "The Lord commanded it *by his example* that they might observe it with greater piety."[16] In that statement we have an indication of Calvin's view that the mandate of Sabbath observance is grounded in creation, or, that is, that the Sabbath is a creation ordinance. Richard Gaffin has seen the importance of that for the interpretation of Calvin. He echoes what we shall see below as the conclusion of John Murray on the point. Gaffin's conclusion is that "The notion of the Sabbath institution as a creation ordinance... although not explicitly stated, is consonant with and perhaps even implied in the teaching of the *Institutes*."[17]

There is no anti-Sabbatarianism, but, quite to the contrary, what Gaffin refers to in another context as Calvin's "practical Sabbatarianism,"[18] in the following extract from Calvin's sermons on Deuteronomy: "We must refrain from our own business which might hinder us from the minding of God's works; and we must call upon his name and exercise our selves in his words. If we spend the Lord's Day in making good cheer, and in playing and gaming, is that a good honoring of God? Nay, is it not a mockery, nay a very unhallowing of his name? Yes. But when the shopwindows are shut in on the Lord's Day, and men travel not as they do on other days, it is to the end that we should have more leisure and liberty to attend to the things that God commandeth... But most folk have no regard at all to the using of that day, which was ordained to withdraw us from all earthly cares and affairs that we might give our selves wholly unto God."[19]

---

16. Ibid., 396, italics added.
17. Gaffin, *Market Day*, 31.
18. Ibid., 109.
19. Calvin, Sermon 34 on Deuteronomy, cited in Dennison, *Market Day*, 7, spelling modernized. A recent translation of this sermon is contained in *John Calvin's Sermons on the Ten Commandments*.

THE SABBATH OBLIGATION

The Sabbath as God's day

As we recognize now God's establishing the Sabbath day, its meaning and significance and its place in doctrinal theology, we can profitably reflect on some preliminary issues.[20] The first is implicit in what has been said. The Sabbath day is God's day. It is a creation entity which, together with its antitypical expectation, is characterized by covenantal perpetuity. It is an element of the total reality external to the Godhead that God spoke into existence, the purpose and objective of which was the glorification of God throughout the ensuing and eternal ages. It cannot be overstated that all that was created—time as a mode of finite existence, material reality and the laws of its operation, the laws of reason and right understanding, and human personhood—is God's property. He is therefore able to dispose of all such entities according to his will. The disposition of times and seasons and days, and of the history of what has been made, lies completely within the prerogatives of God's decretive will. That prerogative extends to the purpose and intention of his own holy day. He has made abundantly clear his intention in making his holy Sabbath available to us and in clarifying his purpose and will in doing so.

In an approach to the doctrine of the Sabbath, the words with which Warfield began his essay referred to in the preceding footnote are relevant: "I am to speak to you today," Warfield says, "not of the usefulness or of the blessedness of the Sabbath, but of its obligation. And I am to speak to you of its obligation, not as that obligation naturally arises out of its usefulness or blessedness, but as it is immediately imposed by God in His Word."

An approach to the doctrine of the Sabbath necessarily turns on two important issues that are projected by what has been said to this point. First, it is necessary to reflect on certain implications of what has been referred to as the createdness of time and, thereby, of the Sabbath day as a created entity characterized by unique and special purposes in the divine decree. It will follow that the Sabbath, as a result, is to be understood as a *creation ordinance*. Its primary importance and its primary import for

---

20. The classic Puritan work on the doctrine of the Sabbath is Nicholas Bownd, *The True Doctrine of the Sabbath*. A valuable edition with introduction and analysis by Chris Coldwell has been published by Reformation Heritage Books, 2015. For modern treatments see McGraw, *The Day of Worship*. A valuable treatment of Calvin's view of the Sabbath is Gaffin, *Calvin and the Sabbath*. See also Murray, "The Sabbath Institution." An important earlier treatment is Warfield, "The Foundations of the Sabbath in the Word of God," an address given at the Fourteenth International Lord's Day Congress in Oakland, California in 1915.

human conduct are not to be understood as following from God's *redemptive* decree, but from his *creative* decree. That statement should not be taken to mean that there is no relation at all between the mandate of Sabbath observance and the objectives of God's redemptive-eschatological purpose. We shall return to that relation below. The pre-fall Sabbath, like the tree of life, had sacramental significance, and as such it contained within it the promise of eternal rest to which it pointed. But the meaning of the Sabbath as it is presented to us in the revelation as a whole is understandable firstly, not under the rubric of redemption, but under that of creation. That realization will be seen to point to the continuity in time of the creation-Sabbath mandate. That important fact has not, however, been universally recognized. The understanding of the Sabbath as a creation ordinance has been vigorously contradicted, for example by Jay Adams in his *Keeping the Sabbath Today*.[21] Adams claims that Christians should not keep the Sabbath because, as he argues, the Sabbath is a Jewish holy day. Romans 14 and Colossians 2, it is said, demonstrate that Jewish holy days are not binding on Christians, and therefore "the Bible teaches that the Sabbath has been abolished."

We shall return to the meaning and relevance of God's creation ordinances, notably that of the Sabbath along with the ordinances of marriage and work, and their abiding relevance for human conduct and affairs. But for the present, it will throw necessary light on our discussion to reflect on the second of the preliminary issues to be raised; namely, the state of man as he came from the hands of his Creator and the relevance of that to his recognition that God had established his own holy day as a part of his creation. Adam knew at the same time, it will be argued, that he was under the requirement to keep that day, as a day of worship, holy to God.

Man as he was created was the image of God. It is necessary to expand on that important point of doctrine because, interested as we are in the doctrine of the Sabbath, we are required to ask at the beginning who it is on whom God has laid the obligations of the Sabbath. And adequate progress will be made only as the answer is clear that those obligations are laid on man as the image of God. Let us therefore expand on that answer, and on why we state, not that man *bears* the image of God but that he *is* the image

---

21. Adams in *Keeping the Sabbath*. See McGraw, Review of *Keeping the Sabbath*, 275–81.

I am indebted for this reference to Ryan M. McGraw, *The Day of Worship*, ebooks edition, 307–308.

of God. And it is, then, that image of God on whom, as we have said, the obligations of the Sabbath that we shall go on to discuss are laid.

When Adam came to self-consciousness he knew with an uncluttered naturalness that he was the being of a Creator-God. For Adam, to *be* was to *know*. The *imago Dei* carried with it extensive ontological and epistemic implications. For Adam, a rational, immortal, spiritual, moral, and speaking being, endowed with faculties of soul, of intellect, emotion, and will, and endowed above all creation with the capacity for speech, his prelapsarian relations with God were of unique character and import. In his initial state man, with a natural self-consciousness, knew that he had come from the hands of a Creator-God. As the image of God, man thinks and speaks because God thinks and speaks, he loves because God loves and is love, he acts with reflective volition because God acts, first in the work of creation and then in the works of providence and redemption. In his initial state of intrinsic holiness man, in the exercise of his intellectual faculty, naturally knew God, with his affective faculty he naturally loved God, and with his volitional faculty he naturally obeyed the will of God. There was then a naturalness in Adam's relation with God that was lost forever at the fall, except it should be regained by the renewing, regenerating grace of God. That naturalness of relation meant that Adam naturally thought God's thoughts after him.

Adam thought and spoke because God thought and spoke. He was a moral entity because God is moral. He was immortal in soul because God had conferred derivative immortality on him. Adam was constituted in derivative personhood because absolute personhood resides in God. He was the analogue of God as to both his being and knowledge. To say that man is the image of God is to say that he is like God in every respect in which a finite person can be like his infinite Creator. All that points, precisely, to our first parent's natural consciousness of his initially-constituted Sabbath obligations.

It is that, we shall see more fully, that established Adam's cognizance that the Sabbath was what we have referred to as a creation ordinance. If it were to be said, as has been frequently observed, that it is nowhere stated in the early chapters of Genesis that man was obligated to observe one day in seven as God's holy day, the response is clear. In his initial state, as has been said, Adam knew (in analogical extent and within the capacities of his finitude) that God rested on the seventh day and that a pattern was thereby established that was to determine his own behavior. Adam, we have said, naturally knew and thought the thoughts of God after him.

The early-nineteenth-century Scottish theologian, Patrick Fairbairn, has observed insightfully to the same effect: "True, indeed, we are often told, there was no formal enactment binding the observance of the day on man; there is merely an announcement of what God did, not a setting forth to man of what man should do; it is not said that the Sabbath was expressly enjoined upon man. And neither, we reply, should it have been; for, since man was made in the image of God, it was only, so long as this image remained pure, the general landmarks of moral and religious duty which were required for his guidance, not specific and stringent regulations; for he had the light of Heaven within him, and of his own account should have taken the course which his own circumstances, viewed in connection with the Divine procedure, indicated as dutiful and becoming."[22]

In a valuable section on "Creation ordinances" in his *Principles of Conduct*, the mid-twentieth-century Reformed theologian John Murray concurs in his observation that "The argument commonly advanced is that the silence of Genesis on the matter of the Sabbath indicates that there was no weekly Sabbath in patriarchal times and that it was first instituted after the Exodus. Genesis is not silent. Genesis 2:2, 3 proves that the Sabbath is a creation ordinance and, as such, must have been known to Adam and his contemporaries. The silence of Genesis subsequent to Genesis 2:2, 3 proves nothing as to the desuetude of the institution during the patriarchal times, nor does it prove ignorance of the ordinance on the part of the patriarchs."[23] John Murray has illumined the controversies that swirl in the consideration of our subject in his essay on "The Sabbath Institution."[24] He addresses insightfully "the *Obligation*, the *Sanctity*, and the *Observation* of the Sabbath." He again insists on the identity and sanctity of the Sabbath as a creation ordinance. "The weekly Sabbath," Murray concludes, "is embedded in that order which God has established for man as man... The fourth commandment simply defined what was the already existing institution."[25] But the objection referred to has attracted a good deal of attention and

---

22. Fairbairn, *Revelation of Law*, 52–53. See also Fairbairn, *Typology of Scripture*, II:461–76, cited in Dennison, *Market Day*, 8.

23. Murray, *Principles of Conduct*, 34–35.

24. Murray, "Sabbath Institution," I:205–18, first published by the Lord's Day Observance Society, London, an address given in 1953.

25. Murray, "Sabbath Institution," I:208.

warrants further brief comment. The word "ordinance" refers, of course, simply to an order of arrangement, a disposition of matters according to rule, without reference to any necessity that the arrangement should be explicitly promulgated in writing. The burden of our argument is that God communicated such a rule to our first parent by reason, as we have said, that Adam, as the prelapsarian analogue of God and in perfect holiness, communed with God and thought the thoughts of God after him.

In his recent and highly valuable book on "The Threefold Division of the Law," (ceremonial, civil, and moral) Philip Ross has judiciously observed the place of the Sabbath obligation within the mandates of the law. He has referred to Tim Keller's recent observation that a number of presbyters in the Presbyterian Church in America, for example, have stated their exception to its statement regarding the Sabbath in their subscription to the *Westminster Confession of Faith*.[26] Ross comments that one cannot "unbuckle the Sabbath" in that fashion without unraveling the whole. "Attempts at performing a precision strike on the Sabbath produce an embarrassing amount of unintended damage. Strike out the Sabbath and you also shatter the entire category of moral law and all that depends on it."[27]

Ross responds, therefore, to the claims that "there is no direct command to keep the Sabbath or give it religious significance in Genesis 2,"[28] citing the claims made in that connection by Harold Dressler.[29] Ross's response, which is worthy of fuller examination in context, aligns with what he concludes as "the view of the confessionists and older writers such as Calvin[30] that the Sabbath was established at creation and known before Sinai."[31]

The Sabbath a creation ordinance and its covenantal significance

Returning now to the second of the two preliminary issues we have raised, the significance of the fact that the Sabbath day was a creation ordinance warrants further brief recognition. The essential meaning of a

26. Ross, *Finger of God*, 5.
27. Ibid., 6.
28. Ibid., 66.
29. See Dressler, "The Sabbath in the Old Testament" in Carson, *Sabbath*, 21.
30. Calvin, *Genesis*, 105–106.
31. Ross, *Finger of God*, 67.

creation ordinance is that because it was addressed to man in his initial and prelapsarian state, it carries with it obligations that accrue to man as man. That is to say, as previously stated, the obligations for human conduct that are projected by creation ordinances do not fall primarily under the rubric of redemption. In God's administration they are free from the considerations of God's *redemptive* purpose, except, as will be seen, that the law was promulgated in redemptive context. The law as given in codified form by Moses, is to be understood as the republication of the law as first given to Adam. That implies, what is of serious import for our study of the Sabbath, that the law of the Sabbath, like all creation ordinances simply because they are *creation* ordinances, is binding and obligatory on all men everywhere and at all times. Keeping the Sabbath day holy is to be seen as an obligation that rests on all people at all times. That is to say, the obligation to keep God's Sabbath holy is not to be understood as incumbent only on the church or on Christian people. By the very nature of its creational-covenantal identity, God calls for its honoring by all people and by the world in general. That implies that economic arrangements, organization, and practices that violate God's clear Sabbath mandate should be brought under reconsideration.

When we refer to the Sabbath day as a covenantal institution we are conscious that differences of view have arisen historically as to the respects in which God's initial relations with our first parents are to be construed in covenantal terms. Is it to be said, for example, that man is to be understood as a covenant creature by reason of his creation, or were the terms of his covenantal relation to God established and communicated to him only after his creation? It is not necessary to enter that argument extensively at this point. But by reason of what has been said regarding the knowledge capacity and complex in which Adam came to self-consciousness, it can be concluded that he was conscious of a covenantal relation existing between himself and his Creator. The present writer is comfortable with the statement that man is a covenant creature and that the covenantal obligations incumbent on Adam at the beginning continue on all people at the present time. It is that continuity which, in one of its aspects, argues for both our first parent's awareness of his Sabbath obligation and the continuity of it.

Consider, for example, what has been referred to in theological terms as the covenant of creation or the covenant of works. It is sufficient for our present purpose to observe that the obligation of keeping the Sabbath day holy, in the worship and adoration of God and in thankfulness to him, was an essential part of the obligations of that covenant. Now it is a critically important part of theological doctrine that the terms and responsibilities inherent in the covenant of works were not abrogated when Adam fell. That the obligations that accrue to man under the covenant of works are of continuing significance, and that they embody a continuing imperative, is evident from the following. First, those who at the last day go to eternal perdition will do so on the grounds that they have not honored the terms and kept the obligations of the covenant of works. Second, it follows that impressed upon us at that point is the reason for the coming into the world of the Second Person of the Godhead as Jesus Christ for our redemption. The purpose of his coming can, of course, be stated in many terms. But in our present context it is to be said that he came to do for us what we were obligated to do under the covenant of works but could not do for ourselves by reason that we were the captives and slaves of Satan and sin. Jesus Christ, in his redemptive accomplishment, is our substitute in every relevant respect. We were associated with him in all that he did on our behalf.

It is in terms such as those, then, the continuity of covenant obligation, that the meaning and significance of God's Sabbath day is to be approached. It cannot be gainsaid or argued against that keeping the Sabbath day holy is obligatory on all people everywhere at all times. That is because, like the covenant of works, it was established as part of man's prelapsarian obligation, and as a creation ordinance its obligation has not been, and could not be, annulled. The Sabbath day, we said at the beginning, has covenantal perpetuity. It is in that same respect that it is necessary to say that all other creation ordinances, in particular marriage and work, continue as imperatively obligatory on all people everywhere at all time. Therein lies our response to the contemporary social and cultural dissolution, particularly that stemming from revisionist theories of marriage.

The use of the Sabbath

In any reasonably comprehensive attempt to examine the doctrine of the Sabbath it is necessary to address at length the manner in which, as God's people, we are to be occupied on the Sabbath day. We have referred to the "covenantal perpetuity" of the Sabbath. We insist, accordingly, on the responsibility of God's people and the church as a confessing church to preserve the sanctity of the Sabbath day. The scriptural *locus classicus* statement on the point is undoubtedly Isaiah 58:13–14, "If thou turn away

Belief and Evangelism

thy foot from the Sabbath, from doing thy pleasure on my holy day, and call the Sabbath a delight, the holy of the Lord, honourable; and shalt honour him, not doing thine own ways, nor finding thine own pleasure, nor speaking thine own words; Then shalt thou delight thyself in the Lord; and I will cause thee to ride upon the high places of the earth, and feed thee with the heritage of Jacob thy father; for the mouth of the Lord hath spoken it." Similarly, it is to be borne in mind that, as Calvin observes, "The Lord enjoined obedience to no other commandment as severely as to this."[32] The relevant texts are copious and the principal burden of them is to the effect: "Blessed is the man that keepeth the Sabbath from polluting it" (Isa 56:2), and as in Nehemiah 9:14, God's jealousy is for his "holy Sabbath."[33]

The exegesis of the texts could detain us at length.[34] But it lies behind the question and answer of the Catechism: "How is the Sabbath to be sanctified?" "The Sabbath is to be sanctified by a holy resting all that day, even from such worldly employments and recreations as are lawful on other days; and spending the whole time in the public and private exercises of God's worship, except so much as is to be taken up in the works of necessity and mercy."[35] The Catechism, of course, is a production of the Puritan period of history, written in 1647, some half a century after the classic work of Nicholas Bownd referred to in an earlier footnote, and many Christians, and perhaps the church at large in this time, have registered difficulty in subscribing to that earlier interpretation of the biblical data. But it lies on the very surface of the biblical text, and it is clear in the frequent prophetic rebukes of God's people, that God is most jealous for the protection and proper use of his Sabbath day. The failure of the "church in the wilderness" (Acts 7:38) to honor the Sabbath day, along with the peoples' idolatry and spiritual adultery, was a recurring ground of charge against them.

But if there has developed in the church at the present time a laxity of regard for the Sabbath in what we have just seen as the older or Puritan sense, the burden lies on the church, and on Christian people in general, to justify such deviations in the light of the more copious biblical data than can be, or need to be, rehearsed at this point. The conclusion to be drawn from those data is that God has said repeatedly that he requires his redeemed

---

32. Calvin, *Institutes*, 395.

33. See Nehemiah 10:31 and 13:15–22 for the insistence on the sanctity of the sabbath and the complaint against its violation by commercial transactions.

34. See the comments on Calvin's exegesis of relevant texts in Gaffin, 86–109.

35. *Westminster Shorter Catechism*, Question 60.

The Sabbath Obligation

people to honor and sanctify his holy Sabbath day, and to devote it exclusively to works, as our fathers in the faith put it, of piety, necessity, and mercy.[36] There is every reason to conclude that God is not pleased with a partial acknowledgement of his Sabbath mandate, or with the importations of alien behavior or thought-forms of the world into the recognition of his day. It is only too true that we have given the idioms of the world hospitality in the church, not only to the diminution of its doctrinal integrity but to the corruption also of its worship forms and content. It is a challenge of the highest import to us at this time to work out the true nature of worship as God has stated it in his Word and to recall scrupulously the necessary occasions of it. We do well to reconsider the manner of our subscription to the Regulative Principle of Worship; not in the patently erroneous form that argues that anything not forbidden by the Word of God is acceptable and proper in worship, but, to the contrary, in the acknowledgement that only that is to be accorded a place in worship which God has required in his Word.

But the approach to the matter of Sabbath-keeping has been very various, and even some theologians of purportedly Reformed persuasion, as in the case, for example, of Jay Adams as referred to earlier, have argued that keeping the Sabbath day holy is not now obligatory on Christians. While a comprehensive analysis cannot be attempted in the present space, a number of comments can be made regarding the starting points under which relevant questions are addressed.

First, on an individual level, discussion frequently begins by asking the question as to what is or is not a proper use of time on the Sabbath day. The question itself is, of course, in its own place, quite proper and important. But what we are speaking of at present is not the rightness of such a question in and of itself, but whether it provides a proper and adequate *starting point* for the examination of the meaning and necessities of the Sabbath day. Quite apart from the acknowledgement that in some degree, to a greater or lesser extent, attendance at worship is required, the question then is whether this or that, depending on individual habits and cultural mores, can also engage one's time. Variations of the relevant argument abound. It is hardly necessary to examine them at length. They have to do with sporting activity, professional or otherwise, on the Lord's day, with economic activity such as shopping (including the purchase of gasoline necessary to attend a house of worship on the Lord's day—an activity

---

36. See the excellent discussion in McGraw, *Day of Worship*.

that might be attended to on the preceding Saturday), and other activities that cater to personal indulgences and proclivities rather than the worship that God calls for. Such questions of personal moment may include those of appropriate reading and engagement in activities related to one's normal worldly responsibilities and occupations, including work and study.

But rather than continue such a listing unnecessarily, it is apposite to observe that a prior question is of pressing significance. If the address to the proprieties of the Sabbath begins in the manner indicated, argument has begun on the wrong track and cannot, therefore, hope to reach a biblically sustainable conclusion. That is because the implied question that begins the journey of inquiry is what is required in the interests of man, rather than what is required in the interests of what God desires and has decreed. Man and his interests are made the center of things. Such argument partakes of the all too frequent fallacy of imagining that thought can rightly proceed from man to God, rather than from God to man. The presence of that fallacy appears in all too many areas of theological doctrine and practice, notably in theological apologetics where assumptions of the competence of human reason lead to what is essentially a theological rationalism. We have just said that the same mistake in thought can intrude into our thinking about the Sabbath if, again, we begin with the interests of man instead of focusing on the interests of God and his clearly mandated requirements. All too frequently, even in the affairs of the church including its theological formations, the thought forms employed have been anthropocentric and not theocentric.

Second, the question of what it is proper for the church to include in its activities on the Sabbath has formed the starting point of inquiry. There is reason to question the propriety of the extent to which the church has given hospitality to activities on the Lord's Day that, on more careful thought, might be seen to offend what God has mandated. In that very sensitive area it is observable that considerable elasticity of permission exists in the contemporary church. Church-sponsored picnics on the Sabbath have been accorded indulgence, and it is not improper to question how that matter stands, or if it should stand, against what we observed as the advice of the Catechism that prohibited on the Sabbath "such employments and recreations as are lawful on other days." But further questions of the proper use of the time and facilities of the church on the Sabbath day, open to sensitive discussion and possibilities of even strong disagreement as they are, require at least recognition. For example, the provision of musical programs that purport to meet primarily the necessities of the worship and glory of God, but which nevertheless are in danger of serving the interests of entertainment, appear to be a case in point.

Third, it is not infrequently advanced as a starting point for discussion that the primary consideration regarding the Sabbath day is that of rest. It is clear, of course, that "God rested on the seventh day." And there can be no doubt at all that God in his gracious provision for man ordained a day of rest from worldly employment and toil. That is for the refreshment of body and spirit. But of course, God's rest as there stated is rest from the work of creation and does not mean total inactivity on God's part. His works of providence and his immanent engagement in human affairs continue. And as we have seen, human work on the Sabbath is mandated continuously as works of piety, necessity, and mercy. And there is no doubt that the rest of the Sabbath day points to the great eschatological terminus when we shall have entered the land of rest and gained the inheritance that God has prepared for those that love him. It is true that God's people have in this life the "earnest" (Eph 1:14), or the down payment, of the inheritance that has been reserved for them. "The promise of eternal inheritance" (Heb 9:15), or the final realization of the inheritance that has been promised, is not only guaranteed to them, but by God's gracious disposition has been made available to them in this present life. The rest that is properly a part of the Sabbath day falls into that category of the taste of better things to come. As the land of Canaan was typical of the eternal land of rest, so the Sabbath is in the same respect typical of the eternal rest that is to come. Again it may be observed that while the Sabbath was made for man (Mark 2:27), the question presses as to why and for what purpose that was so. As we have argued that it was not made for man to do with it as he might wish, but to use it for the worship and praise and honor of God, so we observe in the present context that it was not made for man to use as an occasion of idleness. It was made for man that he might use it in its entirety for the worship and praise of God.

But in spite of all that is properly to be said of the Sabbath as a day of rest, together with all of its projected eschatological significance, our interest at present is whether the concept of rest can, or should, form the primary or principal *starting point* for the examination of the meaning and importance of the Sabbath. Again our answer is in the negative. We do not intend to diminish in any respect the high theological significance of the rest to which the Sabbath points. But we are saying that it is not the *first* or the *primary* issue or question that should decide our approach to understanding the Sabbath day. The concept of rest has its own important and proper place in the scheme of things. But the *first* approach to understanding the Sabbath day lies on another level. It is the fact that God has spoken and has said that he requires of all people everywhere that they should keep one day in seven separate from, distinguished from, all other days, and that that day should be occupied entirely in the worship and praise in honor of, and thankfulness to, God.

Two further points can be made in that connection. First, we have spoken of the necessity laid upon us to keep one day in seven holy to God. It is beyond the scope of our present purpose to address the change of day from the seventh to the first day of the week. Suffice it to say that the change of day honors the day of the resurrection of our Lord, and that the change has proceeded on apostolic authority. Second, if, as has been argued, the matter of the rest that is a proper element of the Sabbath day is elevated to the point of determining or driving what is to be said from that point on, the danger arises as before, and in other connections, that the interests of man are elevated beyond the interests of God and his stated mandates. Again the same possibility is presented of arguing from man to God instead of from God to man. The dangers of such a misdirection of thought need not be repeated.

The law of the Sabbath

Our argument to this point has been based on the postulate that the Sabbath is a creation ordinance. The doctrine of the Sabbath, therefore, falls, as we have said, not under the rubric of redemption but under that of creation. The question arises, however, whether the Sabbath is to be understood as having redemptive-eschatological significance and whether doctrinal significance attaches to the consideration of it under those terms. Our answer is in the affirmative. The reasons for that conclusion have been anticipated in what has been said and can be profitably expanded at this point.

First, what is now to be considered as "the law of the Sabbath" requires that conclusion. When we speak now of the law of the Sabbath we have in view the law in its codified form as it was given through Moses. Several things are to be said in that connection. The Mosaic law, encapsulated so far as our present purposes are concerned in the Ten Commandments or the moral law, is to be understood as the republication of the law in its moral aspect as it was first given to Adam in his prelapsarian state. It is precisely because of that republication, and the status of the law as God delivered it, that we can speak of the covenantal perpetuity of the Sabbath. In the incorporation of the Sabbath law in the Mosaic codification, that perpetuity is exhibited clearly to human understanding. But in saying that, we do not fall into the error of concluding that the Sabbath law, as it was recapitulated by Moses, falls under the denomination of the ceremonial law which, by virtue of its ceremonial qualification, was terminated at the conclusion of the Mosaic administration. We do not erect by such a channel a Christian escape from the spirit and the letter of the Sabbath law commands. Indeed, when the Decalogue says "Remember the Sabbath day," the call is not in the first place to keep on remembering it in the future, keeping it holy, and not letting it slip from one's consciousness. The primary import of the command is that it is the necessary to remember what was given as an established ordinance long ago. Call it to your remembrance in its covenantal obligation.

Second, our Lord himself honored and spoke of the continuity of the Sabbath, speaking of the fact that "Moses and the prophets and the Psalms" spoke of him (Luke 24:44) and he stated that he himself was Lord of the Sabbath (Mark 2:28). Christ thereby brought to high exposure both the covenantal status of the law and the continuity of it, for he himself is Lord of the covenant, and he has called his people to the level of sanctified, holy living that he himself exhibited in his keeping of the law.

Third, by reason that Christ in those ways brought the Mosaic republication of the Sabbath law under the jurisdiction of his new covenantal administration he has magnified the divine intent of the law as it was at first given. That is to say, he has condescended to our finite understanding and cognitive capacity by communicating to us through Moses a detailed guidance as to the fuller meaning and applicability of the law. That was done in order that we should again be like him in our obedience to it; not that the keeping of the law has for us meritorious salvific significance, but that in response to, and thankfulness for, redemption we honor God in obedience to the Sabbath law. It is in the sense of that republication and our Lord's authentication of it that the Sabbath law acquires definite redemptive relevance. That means that in our Lord's new covenantal administration the original creation ordinance is integrated into his total redemptive objectives and purposes. What we are saying in that statement is not that the Sabbath is now to be regarded as having been established as a redemptive ordinance. We are saying that the law of the Sabbath as an unalterable creation ordinance has been integrated with redemptive objectives, provisions, and processes.

Fourth, the conception of the law of the Sabbath as integrable with redemptive-eschatological categories is consistent with what has been said regarding the Sabbath rest in its eternal form to which the law of the Sabbath points.[37] In that connection we observed at the beginning that the creation-Sabbath mandate, like the tree of life, is to be understood as projecting sacramental significance.[38] In both those cases our first parents' experience, their partaking of the fruit of the tree and their engaging in weekly worship, confirmed to them the promise of eternal life and rest that God's eschatological purpose envisaged.[39]

Fifth, it is to be understood that the law as given in its Mosaic codification was the property of the Israelitish nation-church that God had chosen as his peculiar people. They were to be to him a "holy nation" (Exod 19:6). The law in that form was not given to the Gentiles. Indeed, when the apostle stated in his letter to the Galatians that "Christ hath redeemed us from the curse of the law" (Gal 3:13) he had in view the law in its Mosaic formulation (Gal 3:10–12), and the "us" he contemplated referred to the Jews who had become believers. The Gentiles could not be said to have been redeemed from the curse of the Mosaic law because they were never the possessors of that law. Indeed, Paul goes on to state at that point that the reason for the rescue from the curse was "that the blessing of Abraham might come on the Gentiles through Jesus Christ" (Gal 3:14). The "blessing of Abraham" was justification by faith. It was necessary that at that point God's special relation to the Israelitish nation-church should be terminated and the doors of the kingdom thrown wide open to the Gentiles. There was an important respect in which, of course, the Gentiles were redeemed from the curse of law. But the law from whose curse they were redeemed was not the law that had been the property of the Israelites. It was the law that had been given to our first parents at the beginning and which, by reason of its covenantal-creation status, had continued to be binding on all people since its first promulgation. That law, we have seen, contained

---

37. Calvin's emphasis on that aspect of the Sabbath mandate has been noted above.

38. The sacramental significance of the Sabbath has been examined by Vos in *Biblical Theology*, 157, cited in Gaffin, *Calvin and the Sabbath*, 156–57.

39. On the question of the sacramental significance of the tree of life see Turretin, *Institutes*, 1:581.

the obligation to keep God's Sabbath holy. The Gentiles were henceforth bound to the obligations of the Sabbath law, now in its reformulation in new covenantal context. In the one church in which the Jew and the Gentile had met together now that the "middle wall of partition" (Eph 2:14) had been broken down by the salvific work of Christ, the Sabbath law abides with commanding imperative.

Those considerations point to the reality that Christ, by subsuming the original and continuing Sabbath law under the scope of the requirements and benefits and blessings of his new covenantal administration, has made possible the integration of the law of the Sabbath with what we have referred to as redemptive-eschatological categories.

Identity and authority

Our argument at this point returns to a proposition with which we began. Reference was made there to the twofold issues confronting the church at this time as those of *identity* and *authority*. What we have said about the Sabbath, its creation-covenantal status and the continuing imperatives it conveys for Christian life, is readily understandable in the light of those stated issues of identity and authority. For when the confessing Christian knows with a life-determining consciousness who he is by reasons of the status to which he has been raised by the grace of God, he must of necessity rest securely, with a contentment born of divine endowment, under the authority of God who has redeemed him. Identity and authority are coordinate in their import. Because the Christian person is who he is, the moral mandates of God's law command his dedication in devotion and life.

We have spoken of Adam as constituted in the image of God and as cognizant of his covenantal responsibilities. But if our first parent was obliged to, and in the nature of the case committed himself in obedience to, the Sabbath law of God, how much more should that be the joy of the Christian in this time. For consider the relation of identity that exists. The apostle to the Romans has crystallized the issue. In his clarification of the identity of the Christians to whom he wrote, he argued that "Where sin abounded, grace did much more abound" (Rom 5:20). What is involved for the new identity of the Christian, the "new creation" as Paul argued it to the Corinthians (2 Cor 5:17), is that by the grace of God he has been raised to a far higher estate than that from which Adam fell. That is the "more abounding" of grace. The higher estate for the Christian is that he is joined to God in Christ in a vital and indissoluble union. Adam was not joined to Christ in the same respect. We can state the case by saying that as to the unregenerate man, the relation between God and himself is a relation between two independent entities. But in the case of the Christian that is not true. For now he is, with a spiritual literalness, joined to Christ. God abides in him. As our Lord stated, "My Father will love him, and we will come unto him, and make our abode with him" (John 14:23). We note the plural forms of the pronouns. "We," our Lord says, the Father and the Son, implying that the three Persons of the Godhead who live in divine perichoresis, live within the Christian. The concept in its fullest meaning and implication is beyond our comprehension. The apostle John in his first epistle states repeatedly that "God dwelleth in us" (1 John 4:12), and that we are "in him" and "in his Son Jesus Christ" (1 John 5:20). That *identity*, it is now being said, responds to the necessities of *authority*. The Christian knows whose he is and whom, therefore, he serves.

It is not necessary at this stage to expand the argument at length. We may make just one further reference to the expansive literature on this important subject. Walter Chantry, a contemporary Baptist preacher-theologian who has made notable contributions to recent Reformed thought, has thrown valuable light on the issues we have raised in his *Call the Sabbath a Delight*.[40] "What joyful and abundant benefits flow from Sabbath-keeping! Did you not at conversion pledge to keep all the Lord's holy will? Did this not include his moral law and the fourth commandment? After tasting the exquisite generosity of God's grace—not only to pardon our multitude of sins against his law and to admit us again to his service, but also to make us sons and daughters of God, priests and kings with Christ—our hearts should overflow with loving obedience. If it would please him that I kept the Sabbath Day, my heart would run with delight to the task. Oh, to return something to the One who has been infinitely gracious and kind to me! Sabbath observance surely is part of this return of obedience."[41] "Forgiven sinners have received such unbelievably precious gifts from God's hands, by grace through Christ, that they are eager to do something for him. Christians are delighted to keep the Sabbath holy. Sabbath days bring them

---

40. Chantry, *Sabbath*. See 110–112 for a useful guide to the literature on the subject of the Sabbath.

41. Ibid, 73–7.

nearer still to the God they love and who loves them. Their love wants to give obedience and honour to the Lord on his day."[42]

Conclusion

In our foregoing argument and analysis we have not set out to address in the full sense necessary all that is to be said about the biblical doctrine of the Sabbath. We bow in humility and thankfulness and praise before God for his conferring on us, sinners saved by his grace, the blessing of the Sabbath day which, as Isaiah admonished us long ago, we make a delight.

Our conclusion follows that to keep the Sabbath day holy to God as a day devoted to his worship is thus, in a cumulative sense, incumbent on all people everywhere at all times. That follows, first, from what has been observed as the creation ordinance status of the day, and secondly, from the fact that our Lord has assumed the sanctity of the day into the meaning and benefits of his redemptive accomplishment.

---

42. Ibid., 79.

Chapter 8

Oaths and the *Imago Dei*

SOUNDNESS OF CHRISTIAN PERCEPTION on the levels of theological doctrine, such as have engaged us in the preceding chapters, should not be allowed to cloud the fact that the Christian lives in a real-world structure of social and cultural complexes. The church is in the world, but it is not, by reason of the belief systems and the biblical ethic to which it is committed, controlled by the thought forms and behavior norms of the world. The Christian's citizenship is in heaven. But while that is true, until the final day of resolution comes by the grace and in the providence of God, the Christian is under obligation of citizenship in the world of everyday. It follows that an important part of theological investigation has to do with unraveling the lines of relation between Christian belief, on the one hand, and Christian ethics on the other. In his insightful and valuable work on *Principles of Conduct*, John Murray has elucidated many of the lines of contact between those two closely related areas of belief and ethics.[1] It is consistent with the perspectives we have raised in the preceding chapters to state with Murray that "The ten commandments . . . furnish the core of biblical ethics."[2] We have observed, moreover, that the codification of the moral law as inscribed in the Decalogue is properly understood as a republication and rearticulation of the law as it was given to our first parents at the beginning.

With that in view, the present chapter aims to provide an illustration of the linkage that exists between Christian belief and ethical responsibilities. The item selected for discussion by way of example has not, it appears,

1. Murray, *Principles of Conduct*.
2. Ibid., 7.

Oaths and the *Imago Dei*

been subject to very close scrutiny in the theological literature. But the question of the relation between Christian confession and the swearing of oaths has been subject to examination and advice in the confessional documents of the church, such as the *Westminster Confession of Faith* that we have referred to in earlier chapters.

In its chapter 22, "Of lawful oaths and vows," the Confession places before us two directive statements relating to lawful oaths. It is stated, first, that "The name of God only is that by which men ought to swear"; and second, that "to swear vainly, or rashly, by that glorious or dreadful name . . . is sinful, and to be abhorred."[3] In the light of those statements, three questions arise: First, what is to be understood as "the name of God" that is advanced as the only legitimate ground of oath-swearing; second, who, among men, can legitimately establish prerogative in swearing lawful oaths and submitting to the implications of them; and third, in the light of answers to those questions what is to be understood as the mandate against "vain" and "rash" swearing? It will be suggested in the following discussion that the import of those questions is heightened by the recognition of man as *imago Dei*, the image of God; and that the direction in which answers to the questions follow turns on that recognition.

To begin, we take first the question of the *imago Dei*. For purposes of the present discussion it is necessary to recall and apply in new dimension some minimal aspects of previous conclusions. Man, in short, is to be recognized as the derivative analogue of God. Derivative and responsible personhood resides in man because, as Van Til put it, absolute personhood resides in God. When it is said that man is the derivative analogue of God it is meant that man stands in an analogical relation to God on the levels of both his being and his knowledge. That is to say, man is *like* God his Creator, but is not *identical with* God. As to his *being*, man is characterized by finite resemblances of the infinite characteristics of God who created him. Man as he came from the hands of his Creator is like God in every respect in which a finite and initially holy entity can reflect in his personhood the infinite excellencies of God. Then further, man is the derivative analogue of God as to his *knowledge* and epistemic capacities in that his knowledge is analogical of the knowledge that God possesses in himself. That is to say,

---

3. The same statements are contained in the *Savoy Declaration of Faith* and in the *Second London (Baptist) Confession*.

man is able to possess *true* knowledge of what God knows and has revealed, but he is not able to possess *comprehensive* knowledge.[4]

God alone, in his eternal infinity, knows all of the relations between all objects of knowledge. Man, the image of God, can know or comprehend in his finitude only parts and aspects of those relations. Further, God knows all things because he thought all things in one eternal moment before the foundation of the world. God spoke into existence all reality external to the Godhead and all the laws of operation of that reality, including the laws of thought.

Human personhood, then, discloses no higher connotation than that described by the fact that God created man in his own image. Man is a covenant creature. Endowed with faculties of soul that are derivative of divine being and essence, our first parent, as he came to self-conscious awareness, realized that he mirrored in finite degree the character of his divine Creator. When God said "Let us make man in our image" (Gen 1:26), the "us" in the speech of God was not an address to "his angelic court," notwithstanding some current theological opinion to that effect.[5] Nor is the "us" simply a use of the royal plural. Already at the beginning of the record of God's revelation we have, along with the "Spirit" in Genesis 1:2, an intimation of the trinity of the Godhead and the relations within it. Those relations require us to acknowledge the perichoresis of the Godhead (the indwelling of the Persons of the Godhead in one another) and further issues that cannot detain us at this time.

It follows that in the status in which he was established, in soulish faculties of intellect, emotion, and will, Adam thought and spoke because God thinks and speaks; with a naturalness he knew God and knew that he had come from the hands of God; Adam loved God with a naturalness because God loves and is love; man is a moral entity because God is moral;

---

4. The distinction that has just been drawn propels our thought to an important question that deserves the closest attention on the level of theological prolegomena, the detailed discussion of which is beyond our present intention. That is the distinction between *archetypical* theology and *ectypal* theology. The former refers to God's knowledge of himself and his works, and the latter refers to creaturely knowledge of God and his works available to man by reason of God's revelatory communication. That distinction and its importance in early post-Reformation theology appears to have been first expressed prominently in the work of Franciscus Junius, in *De theologia vera* in 1594. Its continued importance is reflected in Berkhof's *Systematic Theology*, 35, "Alongside the archetypal knowledge of Him [God], found in God Himself, there is an ectypal knowledge of Him, given to man by revelation."

5. Waltke, *Old Testament Theology*, 127.

and with a naturalness Adam obeyed God. In summary terms we can state the following:

> "Man, created soul and body, male and female, is the *image of God* in that he is a *rational, immortal, spiritual, moral,* and *speaking* person, capable of *reflective self-awareness* and *purposive action*, characterized in his created condition by *knowledge* and by *constitutive righteousness,* and endowed with the capacity for the reception of divine revelation, social relations and communication, and communion with God his Creator."[6]

As we proceed to questions of ethical responsibilities, it is necessary to be alert to the fact that the image of God in man was marred by Adam's fall, in that he lost his initially endowed knowledge, righteousness, and holiness. But while that is so, it remains true that man is still the image of God in that he is still a rational, immortal, spiritual, moral, and speaking person (Gen 9:6; Jas 3:9). At this time, it can be said that man as the image of God sustains two essential relations to God. First, he is the beneficiary of the blessings of God's common grace. But as history continues, common grace will diminish, and at the crack of doom, at the final day, it will have come to an end. Second, by reason of the obligations laid upon him by the primeval covenant of works, sometimes referred to as the covenant of creation, man remains subject to those obligations and will in due time be judged on the grounds of his obedience to them. For the love of God is coordinate with the wrath of God, and divine justice responds to human accountability. God loves all men as creatures, but he hates the sinner as a sinner. "God is angry with the wicked every day" (Ps 7:11), or as another translation has it, God "feels indignation every day."

The plan of argument

The statement of the *Westminster Confession* that "The name of God only is that by which men ought to swear,"[7] brings together the matter of oath-swearing by both God, on the one hand, and man as the derivative analogue of God on the other. The argument that follows will accordingly address, in briefer terms than are warranted, three loosely related issues: First, if, as has been said, man is the derivative analogue of God, to what

---

6. Vickers, *Christian Confession*, 40–41.
7. *Westminster Confession of Faith*, XXII:2.

extent and in what ways is man's integrity in oath-swearing related to the oath that God himself has sworn? Second, what, essentially, is involved in the oath that God swore? And third, to what extent is man's competence in oath-swearing dependent on the regenerate status or otherwise of the individual swearing the oath? Those questions follow immediately from what has been seen as the relations that exist between man's *being* as the image of God, his resulting *knowledge* and knowing capacities, and his implied *ethical* obligations.

In order to set the stage for further examination of the relations we have just adduced, it is necessary to clarify briefly an aspect of the relations between man's *being*, his *knowledge*, and his *ethical* responsibilities and actions. For as will emerge, it is on the level of ethics that the rightness or otherwise of oath-swearing is to be evaluated. For as to man in his existential status and faculties of intellect, emotion, and will, being (ontology) is prior to knowledge (epistemology), and being and epistemology are prior to right behavior and practice (ethics). If, then, man is *like* God as to his being in analogical and finite relation, and if he knows analogically what God knows and has said, man is to be like God in his actions as well as being. By that it is meant that because all of God's deliberations, actions, and ordinances are righteous, so the actions of man, his image, are to be righteous. That, it will become clear, points to the fact that as God's oath-swearing was righteous, so man's oath-swearing is properly to be righteous. We consider, then, the righteous oath that God swore in the establishment of his covenant with our father Abraham.

A further preliminary point might be noted. It has been said that the analogical relation between man and God requires that as God's actions are righteous, so, also, should be the actions of man who is his image. But that calls in question the meaning of "righteous," particularly as that is relevant to our present context. God, it is clearly revealed, is holy, and God is righteous. But holiness and righteousness, while in important respects they are coterminous, are not synonymous. Holiness, in its essential meaning, refers to the *state* in which an entity exists. It has to do with the character or quality of being. Righteousness, on the other hand, refers to action or conduct or behavior that is consistent with that preceding state. The detailed implications of that important difference do not need to be worked out at present. But essentially, it is meant that righteous action is itself completely distanced and differentiated from all that partakes, or could potentially partake, of anything that is unworthy of the sanctity of the state of holiness that characterizes the person taking the action, or that potentially violates that state.

It follows that in the matter of oath-swearing, the implications of the oath must in every respect be consistent with the state of rectitude claimed by the one who has sworn the oath. Complete integrity, then, demands not only that honesty of intention is of the essence of the oath sworn, but honesty of fulfillment of the implied terms of the oath should follow as might become necessary. In short, that necessary relation and implication means that when an oath is sworn, the one who swears is thereby undertaking that he swears to his own potential hurt, or, as will become clear, to his self-malediction.

The oath of God

The author of the letter to the Hebrews[8] refers to God's covenant with Abraham and states that "When God made promise to Abraham, because he could swear by no greater, he swore by himself... Wherein God, willing to show unto the heirs of promise the immutability of his counsel, *confirmed it by an oath*" (Heb 6:13, 17, italics added). It should be noted that the statement at that point in the letter to the Hebrews is taken from Genesis 22:16, at which point God, in confirming his covenant with Abraham after Abraham has expressed his willingness to offer up his son Isaac in sacrifice, states that "By myself I have sworn."

God's initiative is similarly observed in the record at Genesis 15:9–17, when God, in a unique manner, gave confirmatory evidence to Abraham of his, God's, unswerving faithfulness to the terms of his covenantal promise. The facts related to God's swearing his oath of faithfulness to Abraham are well-known. As it is recorded, God instructed Abraham to take certain animals and, having divided them into parts in a manner instructed, to lay the parts side by side. Then follows a remarkable theophany. God, as a "burning lamp passed between the pieces" (Gen 15:17). God was there acting in a manner that was common to oath-confirmation at that time, swearing an oath of faithfulness to Abraham and to the covenant that he had established with him. In the action that occurred we note the divine unilateral proceedings. It was God who passed between the animal parts in the tradition

---

8. I leave aside the question of the authorship of the letter to the Hebrews. I would not raise any objection if authorship were attributed to the apostle Paul. An extended discussion of the authorship is included in Hughes, *Hebrews*, 19–30.

of oath-swearing, not Abraham. Abraham was the one who was the beneficiary of the covenant. God was there swearing an oath of faithfulness, saying in effect that if he were not faithful to his covenantal promises then let him not be God. Involved in that was God's oath of self-malediction. It was not, at that specific point, that Abraham was called upon to be faithful; it was God's declaring his own faithfulness.

The ground of assurance of covenantal fidelity at that point was the fact that God swore the oath by his own name. "He swore by himself" (Heb 6:13). That, to recall previous argument, was God's righteous action consistent with his own character of holiness. When it is said that there we see God's oath of self-malediction, God is swearing to his own eternal consistency and constancy. At that point, then, a highly relevant correspondence between the divine and human oath-swearing comes into view. God swore by his name. And the statement of the *Westminster Confession* that we have under review states that "the name of God" is the sole ground by which men should swear, in instances where oath-swearing is both called for in human affairs and is legitimate. The relationship underlines the fact that God swore by his name and that consequently, and in view of man's analogical relation to God, his competence in oath-swearing again rests on his swearing by the name of God. The conjunction that is thereby at issue can be observed more fully in the following respects. To observe the connection, it is necessary to recall our starting point, the fact that man has been established as the image of God.

Now the fact that man is the image of God and that he is therefore the derivative analogue of God, and that as to his being he is *like* God though he is not *identical with* God, carries with it certain imperative obligations. Ontology, the question of being, as we have looked at it in the case of the God-man relation and its analogy of being, is prior to, and it gives birth to, and it fills out the meaning of, epistemology or the question of knowing, and ethics. That means more specifically that the priority of being over knowledge rests on the further fact that it is only because God has established the world and all its laws of operation that knowledge of anything is possible. It is the being and reality of God and his decreed ordering of all things that makes it possible to predicate meaning to any aspect of reality or any development within it. It is possible to know anything truly only if one knows God truly. In that ultimate sense, and on the part of man, regeneration, as we shall examine it, is prior to knowing.

That last statement will be seen to be integral with the competence of human oath-swearing, and it projects its implications to the issue that is now before us. For it follows that man is to swear, whenever the occasion of legitimate oath-swearing arises, *by the same name as that by which God himself swore.* That is true precisely because man, who is *imago Dei*, the image of God, is to be like God. That necessary likeness again, in analogical status, decision, and action, establishes what is required for verisimilitude in oath-taking.

We have said that ontology, the question of being, is prior to epistemology, the question of knowing, and that one knows anything truly only as he knows God truly. Being, knowing, and ethics stand in the order we have indicated. That, to recall, brings into focus the ethical imperatives of human decision and action. In short, because, as has been argued, man is like God in his analogical status, so he is to be like God in his conduct or, that is, on the level of ethical behavior. As God is righteous in swearing, so man is to be righteous in swearing. That is the issue in its shortest terms. Oath-swearing that is not only legitimate in itself as to its occasion, but is honestly conducted, partakes of the level of righteousness that reflects the righteousness of God.

That is saying in effect that the swearing of an oath involves at the human level the analogue of the self-malediction that God himself spoke in his oath of covenantal faithfulness. Oaths involve promises, at a minimum level the promise to be truthful. It involves, then, the implied understanding that in the same manner as God placed his own identity and veracity at issue in swearing his oath, so an individual who swears an oath is thereby placing himself at a level of obligation corresponding, on an analogical level, to the obligation that God himself assumed. The oath at the human level acquires its most significant meaning when it is seen as the oath sworn by the image of God, the *imago Dei*.

The relevance of regeneration

What has now been said points to the third of the issues we raised at the beginning. In answering the questions involved at that point, we turn to further comment on the criteria of rightness in knowledge and behavior. We have confronted the question of man's integrity in oath-swearing and the criteria of decision and action that are involved in it. We summarized much of what is to be said in that regard by tracing briefly the relations between, as we put it, being, knowledge, and behavior. Given that the question of being, or of human status, has been resolved in the manner we have indicated, a question follows regarding the correct or true criteria of truth and validity in knowledge. God had placed Adam in possession of the correct and the truly productive criteria on the level of knowledge. He had commissioned Adam to the offices of prophet, priest, and king. But it is one of the many ways of relating the effects and implications of the fall to say that at the fall man lost those true criteria of truth and understanding. Henceforth, in his fallen condition he would derive his criteria of truth and validity from within himself, or from within his surrounding social and cultural milieu. That, in short, is a principal result of the fall. Man henceforth set out to live on the assumption of his autonomy from God, and that false assumption of autonomy has determined his conception of what we have so far seen as his being and his knowledge.

But beyond that is the question of the proper criteria of truth in ethics and behavior. In a way similar to what we have already encountered, man in his fallen condition has rejected the God-given criteria of right behavior and has established his criteria of conduct from within his own imagination or from, again, what is determined by his social and cultural milieu. Such is the sorry and misdirected condition of man in sin. Such are the sorry bequests of the erroneous assumption of human autonomy. But to the contrary, what is now before us requires it to be said that only God and his ethical decrees can establish all such necessary and relevant criteria, not any conceptions born of the assumptions of human autonomy. To project the significance of that conclusion to our present inquiry, it follows that the criteria of rightness and adequacy in oath-swearing must be what God had required and mandated.

But the ability or the willingness to commit to those mandates turns, as must now be seen, on the status of the individual who is confronted by the possibility of oath-swearing. What we are concerned with at that point is the question of the human status and potential for belief and behavior as man stands before the face of God. We observe, therefore, that there are only two classes of people in the world, those who by the regenerating grace of God have been redeemed from the curse of sin and sinful estrangement from God, and those who remain in the darkness of sin and subjection to the god of this world.

Let us put the issue in briefest terms as follows. Everything depends for the question of the competence and propriety of oath-swearing on whether the individual under contemplation is, or is not, the beneficiary of the regenerating grace of God that brings to effect the new vision and new commitment to godly ethical criteria we have referred to. Regeneration, it can be said by way of explanation, is that secret, sovereign, and unsolicited work of the Holy Spirit whereby the individual's faculties of soul are endowed with abilities and capacities they did not previously possess and a new disposition or principle of action is planted within the soul. As the apostle to the Colossians stated it, some, by that sovereign work of the Holy Spirit, have been "delivered from the power of darkness and translated into the kingdom of [God's] dear Son" (Col 1:13). It was observed that at the fall man lost his possession of the true principles and criteria of understanding and of truth and validity in knowledge and behavior. But now, as a result of the new creation that the regenerating grace of the Spirit of God conveys, regeneration recovers for man the true principles of knowledge, understanding, truth, and conduct.

In, then, that regeneration establishes a new state of being, in which epistemic capacities are now made new by the grace of God, new adherences to correct ethical criterial are possible in action.

For our present purposes, it is important to put what has just been said in the following terms. What, we ask, is man's *summum bonum*, his highest good, in this world? And the answer follows that while it is not now possible to *see* God with the naked eyes of our humanness, it is possible to *know* God. Indeed, in our Lord's high priestly prayer that he prayed in the presence of his disciples on the night on which he was betrayed, he stated to that effect. "This is life eternal," he said, "to *know* thee, the only true God and Jesus Christ whom thou hast sent" (John 17:3, italics added). But who is the man that knows God? The unregenerate person does not know God. He has at times, it is true, a cognition of God, a conviction that the true God exists and, moreover, he knows that he is accountable to God. In the sense of a mere cognition, every man knows that God is. But it is not true that every man *knows* God. Every man knows that God exists. But, it is equally necessary to say, while every man therefore knows *that* God is, he does not necessarily know *who* God is.

It is the knowledge of *who* God is that our Lord referred to in his high priestly prayer. That is the privilege which accrues to the regenerate individual. In the sense that is now before us, the conclusion follows that the regenerate person knows God, and the unregenerate person does not know God. That is the inevitable conclusion of a true biblical anthropology.

What, then, is the name of the true God that only the regenerate Christian knows? The name of God, as to the form of address that is warranted, is variously stated in the Scriptures. That is well-known. But our interest at this point is in the fact that the *name* of God means, and stands for, and carries with it the infinite perfections that belong to God as God. To know the *name* of God, therefore, is to be conscious, in the analogical respect that we observed at the beginning, of some aspect of those infinite perfections.

But what is to be said at the same time of the unregenerate person? In the important respect that now engages us, the unregenerate man does not know the name of God. That, now, determines our approach to the highly important question of the swearing of oaths that the *Westminster Confession* has brought to our attention. In short, *if the unregenerate person does not* know *the name of God, how, then, can he* swear *by the name of God?* To suggest that he can would seem to commit a category mistake. Or to put that in another way, what can the unregenerate oath-swearer be imagined to do when he is swearing *by the name of God*? The question would seem to be not unimportant. Should it be concluded that the person who does not know the name of God is in reality, if he swears by the name of God, thereby "taking the name of God in vain" and is forthrightly guilty of breaking the third commandment of the Decalogue?

There are many respects in which the answer to that question would appear to be in the affirmative. But we may look at the case a little more fully. The question is to be considered in the light of the statement in the *Westminster Confession* that "A lawful oath is a part of religious worship."[9] That is underlined by the statement that follows, that the person swearing the oath is understood to be "swearing solemnly" and "calleth God to witness what he asserteth or promiseth."[10] What, it can properly be asked, is the meaning and import of that sentence? The history of commentary has not provided a clear and uniform response to the question. Charles Hodge observes in that connection that the *Thirty-Nine Articles* of the Church of England include comparable words, stating that the swearing of an oath "is to be done in justice, judgment and truth."[11] Charles Hodge, however, observes that "There does not seem to be sufficient reason for this

---

9. *Westminster Concession of Faith*, XXII:1. See also Hodge, C. *Systematic Theology*, 3:310.

10. *Westminster Confession*, XXII:1.

11. See Thomas, *Principles of* Theology, 483.

restriction."[12] Hodge's intention by his argument on the point is not immediately clear, and appearing as it does to miss the claim stated in *Westminster Confession* that is our present concern, it is presented here for purposes of further consideration. "The oath being an appeal to God to bear witness to the truth of our declarations, or the sincerity of our promises, there is no reason why this appeal should not be made whenever any important end is to be accomplished by it."[13]

Prominent in the argument at that point, then, is whether the competence of a person swearing an oath "by the name of God" is confined to those who are regenerate by the grace of God. It is, we have concluded, only such persons who *know* the name of God, and are therefore able righteously to invoke and *swear* by the name of God, who can properly do so. Judgment to that effect would appear to be confirmed by the comment by A. A. Hodge that "It is no less evident that it is dishonest for an atheist to go through the form of swearing at all; or for an infidel to swear with his hand upon the Christian Scriptures, thereby professing to invoke a God in whose existence he does not believe."[14]

The context in which the swearing of an oath is legitimate is illustrated by adequate scriptural data. We are told to swear by the true God, and in doing so to recognize that "A lawful oath consists in calling upon God . . . with an implied imprecation of God's disfavour if we lie or prove unfaithful to our engagements."[15] With that in view, we are told that "Unto me shall every knee bow, every tongue shall swear" (Isa 24:23). And "Thou shalt fear Jehovah thy God, and serve him, and swear by his name" (Deut 6:13). While the oath is thus recognized as a religious institution in the Old Testament, it is to be recognized also that Christ himself was placed under oath by the high priest who said "I adjure thee by the living God," and that he answered accordingly: "Thou hast said." (Matt 26:63–64). The apostle Paul also invoked the name of God in similar contexts: "God is my witness" (Rom 1:9); and "I call God for a record upon my soul" (2 Cor 1:23).

Recall, further, our conclusion when we suggested a definition of the image of God in man. At that point we concluded not that man *bears* the image of God, but that he *is* the image of God. And it was further concluded that notwithstanding man's fall into sin, the image persists. Man is still the

---

12. Hodge, C. *Systematic Theology*, 3:310.
13. Hodge, C. *Systematic Theology*, 3:310.
14. Hodge, A. A., *Confession of Faith*, 287.
15. Ibid.

image of God in the respects we have indicated. That persistence of the reality of image is relevant to our question in further respects. They require us to reflect on man's continuing relation to God and his consequent obligation to God.

Consider God's first covenantal statement of requirement and mandate. That has been generally referred to in theological terms as the covenant of works. The details of its specification do not need rehearsal at this point. But what has to be said is that at the fall the requirements and obligations that man sustains under the terms of that covenant were not abrogated or moderated. Man remains obligated to God under the covenant of works, and if he goes to eternal perdition at last it will be on the grounds that he has not fulfilled the obligations of that covenant.

Now because man remains, in his fallen state, the image of God, and because, as a result, he sustains obligations to God, he is properly committed to the requirements that the *Westminster Confession* has described. That means that all men everywhere are responsible to honor God in life and thought. That includes, notably, in our present context, the swearing of oaths. But in the outcome, it is all too clear that that mandate is not universally honored. Men may swear by the name of God and yet have no conception of the real proprieties of what they purport to be doing. They are then, in their swearing, doing something in ignorance and unbelief. Ignorance is the hallmark of unbelief. The Jews of old who crucified our Lord did so in ignorance. So it is with the unregenerate man who swears in the situation we have just envisaged.

But guilt is not alleviated by ignorance. The man who does not *know* the name of God but yet swears by that name may be ignorantly invoking the true God, simply by reason that the consciousness of the true God, the *sensus deitatis*, lies ineradicably deep within the human soul. If such a person should swear in those terms, he is calling upon himself the potential malediction that unfaithfulness to the requirements of the oath, or the non-performance of its terms, calls for. It would seem that there is reason to conclude that, as is possible also certain of man's sacramental relations to God, the one who swears under those conditions is doing so "unworthily." The same level of unworthiness occurs in the scriptural data in two readily recognizable instances. Understanding that in its essential meaning a sacrament is a confirmation of promise, the tree of life that stood in the garden before Adam's fall is to be understood primarily in its sacramental significance. Though not all theologians agree with the point to be made,

Turretin, for example, who succeeded Calvin following the Reformation, concludes that "The tree is a sacrament and symbol of the immortality which would have been bestowed upon Adam if he had persevered in his first state."[16] Turretin is there in agreement with Augustine on the sacramental significance of the tree of life. Observing on Adam's prelapsarian state, Turretin continues that "As often as he tasted its fruit, he was bound to recollect that he had life not from himself, but from God."[17] When, by reason of his fall into sin, Adam was no longer qualified to partake of the tree, he was excluded, by God's disciplinary action, from access to it. Had he endeavored to return to the garden and eat of the tree he would have done so unworthily and would have called down further damnation on himself.

The second, and comparable, instance of unworthy access to a sacrament applies, as is well known, to unworthy partaking of the sacrament of the Lord's Supper. Again, those in the church who show evidence of being unworthy to participate in the Supper are, by reason of church discipline, excluded from it. Though we are not at this point making any claim for similar sacramental significance of the swearing of an oath, we raise the point of similar unworthiness in engagement in the exercise under review. Oath-swearing "by the name of God" by those who do not *know* the name of God partakes, it is being said, of doing so unworthily and should be shielded from the error itself and the consequences it potentially entails. Such an unworthy action may be taken, as has been said, in ignorance. But again, ignorance does not alleviate guilt.

Conclusion

We have seen that the prime responsibility laid on man is that in every respect he should reflect, in his life and thought, the being, the righteousness, and the perfections of God who has given us his name. Comprehended in that is the fact that the name of God is, for his people, first, the shelter in which they can rest securely in every difficulty and vicissitude; and secondly, it is the basis of rightness in all human action and belief. It is the regenerate person who, by the grace of the Spirit of God that is conveyed in regeneration, can approximate to the high conditions that are involved. For the unregenerate person, that is not so. That is because the unregenerate

---

16. Turretin, *Institutes*, I:581.
17. Ibid.

individual, whether he does so with deliberateness or as a result of blinded ignorance, is living a lie. He not only sees all things "through a glass, darkly" (1 Cor 13:12), but he has, by his involvement in Adam's sin, blinded his eyes so that he willfully cannot see.

We have looked at these and related issues from the perspective of the requirements of oath-swearing. Our conclusion on that level is that serious questions remain as to whether the unregenerate person who does not *know* the name of God in its true connotations is in fact performing an act of treacherous perfidy in claiming to *swear* by that name.

Chapter 9

Conclusion

A SHORT BOOK DOES not need a long conclusion. But it will be useful to recapitulate briefly something of the principal motivation of what has been said to this point and to underline some of the principal conclusions.

First, the church's announced offer of the gospel turns, for legitimacy and consistency, on the specification of its confessional and belief foundations. Attention has been drawn throughout to the extent to which the belief declarations of the church are supportable in the light of biblical data. That has come to prominence in, for example, the awareness of the distinction between the regenerate and the unregenerate man in their respective epistemic competences, in the matter of the knowability of God, and in the ethical obligation laid upon the church and its members.

It is a highly significant aspect of what is involved at such points that a biblically-consistent foundation in apologetic theology should be maintained. It was concluded that a scheme of apologetic foundations referred to as evidentialism argued from a basic postulate of the competence of human reason in the discovery, marshaling, and interpretation of facts. That system of thought argued, in effect, from man to God, and it tended to a theological rationalism. On the contrary, an alternative apologetic thought system, referred to as presuppositionalism and holding to a fundamental apologetic presupposition that *God is* and that he has spoken, argues from God to man. Another way of stating the differences in apologetic perspectives is that while evidentialism places apologetics before theology, the reverse is true for presuppositionalism. In expanding its implications, presuppositionalism understands all of the facts to be God's facts, that it is the meaning of the fact that gives the fact its factness, and that there are no such things as brute, or bare, or uninterpreted facts. All the facts are preinterpreted by God who spoke them into existence, and the task of human inquiry is to *re*interpret, in the light of God's revelation, the *pre*interpreted facts as they exist and are cognizable.

The question of the consistency with which the evangelism of the church proceeds from its foundation in what it understands as its evangel was a principal motivation of all that has been said. In particular, and most notably, the meaning of the sacrificial death of Christ was examined at some length. It was found that having regard to a biblically-consistent statement of the humanness of Christ, the meaning, effect, and salvific significance of his death have not been adequately stated until his suffering on the cross in the soulish aspect of his human nature has been understood and allowed to determine the efficacy of his sacrifice.

Given the nature of man as the image of God, it is to be understood that man is a covenant creature. Indeed, all of God's dealings with man are to be covenantally perceived and interpreted. Similarly, the entire process of redemption that has engaged us from various aspects is to be understood as implementing the covenantal and eternal realities that ensued from the determinate council of the Godhead before the foundation of the world. Under the terms of the covenant of grace, the Second Person of the Godhead came into the world to become Jesus Christ for the redemption of those whom the Father had given to him for that purpose. It is of singular moment that in his coming Christ has done for his people what they were obligated to do under the covenant of works, but what they could not do for themselves by reason that they were bound captive to Satan and sin. The moral and ethical objectives laid on the Christian are similarly to be interpreted in covenantal terms.

Among the objectives and responsibilities of the Christian life, high importance attaches to the keeping of the Sabbath day holy to God. It was found in that connection that the Sabbath requirement is to be understood as a creation ordinance. The interpretation of its meaning and significance, therefore, falls not under the rubric of redemption, but that of creation. A point of considerable importance for human conduct follows. By reason that the Sabbath is a *creation* ordinance, and that it was given to man as man, it remains, along with other creation ordinances, obligatory on all people everywhere and at all time. It is true, of course, as has been emphasized, that the keeping of the Sabbath has, in itself, no salvific effect. The preservation of it responds from the heart of the believer in gratitude to God, who has sanctified the Sabbath, in gratitude for the salvation for sinners that he has set forth in his Son who has referred to himself as "Lord of the Sabbath."

Two observations which in themselves have not been stated explicitly or at length in the preceding chapters call for comment. They have determined the principal concerns that have motivated the work and our all-too-brief resolution of them.

First, the church exists by reason of God's eternally stated purpose and design. We have adverted in that connection to the relevant divine covenantal prescriptions. That being so, a question that needs to be examined at greater length follows: What is the locus of authority, not only for the being of the church, but of its entire confessional foundation and the declaration of it to the world? That authority resides in the word that God has spoken and in the accompanying revelation of himself and his purposes that he has made. That means—and in this lies the issue that deserves more extended discussion than has been accorded it explicitly in the preceding chapters—that that authority is found in explicit formulation in the Scripture that God has given. The church's foundation is the word of God, and the church must stand, therefore, in belief and in practice, on the scripturicity of Scripture. We referred to the word of God as the Christian's Archimedean point.

Second, the corollary follows that in his inscripturated word God has provided for the church all necessary guidance as to its formation, government, belief, and testimony to the world. Further, God has provided his final revelatory guidance in the apostolic deliverance of what our Lord, when he was in this world and then through the enlightenment of his Spirit, gave to the apostles. We have it in Ephesians 2:20 that the church is "built upon the foundation of the apostles and prophets, Jesus Christ himself being the chief cornerstone." In short, the church that declares itself to be the church of God in the world is therefore to be an apostolic church. In the apostolic deliverance and the doctrinal and practical implications that follow from it, God has said his last word to man. As the present writer recalls an outstanding preacher of the twentieth century stating, God has nothing more to say to man that he has not already said.

Bibliography

Abrams, M. H. et al. *The Norton Anthology of English Literature*. New York: Norton, 1962.
Adams, Jay E. *Keeping the Sabbath Today*. Stanley, NC: Timeless Texts, 2008.
Alexander, Cecil Frances. "There Is a Green Hill Far Away." In *Trinity Hymnal*, 256. Atlanta: Great Commissions, 1990.
Auber, Harriet. "Our blest Redeemer, ere He breathed His tender, last farewell." In *Congregational Praise*, 209. London: Independent Press, for the Congregational Union of England and Wales, 1951.
Bahnsen, Greg L. *Van Til's Apologetic: Readings and Analysis*. Phillipsburg, NJ: P&R, 1998.
Berkhof, L. *Systematic Theology*. Grand Rapids: Eerdmans, 1939.
Blanchard, John. *Does God believe in atheists?* Darlington, UK: Evangelical Press, 2000.
Bonar, Andrew A. *A Commentary on Leviticus*. London: Banner of Truth, 1966.
Bownd, Nicholas. *The True Doctrine of the Sabbath*. Grand Rapids: Reformation Heritage Books, 2015.
Bruce, Alexander Balmain. *Apologetics, or Christianity Defensively Stated*. Edinburgh: T. & T. Clark, 1892.
Calvin, John. *Commentary on A Harmony of the Evangelists, Volume First*. Translated by William Pringle. Grand Rapids: Baker, 1979.
———. *Genesis*. Translated by John King. Edinburgh: Banner of Truth, 1975.
———. *Institutes of the Christian Religion*. Translated by Ford Lewis Battles. Edited by John T. McNeill. Philadelphia: Westminster, 1960.
———. *Sermons on the Ten Commandments*. Translated and edited by Benjamin W. Farley. Reprint. Pelham, AL: Solid Ground, 2011.
Carson, D. A. *From Sabbath to Lord's Day*. Eugene, OR: Wipf and Stock, 1999.
Chantry, Walter. *Call the Sabbath a Delight*. Edinburgh: Banner of Truth, 1991.
Charnock, Stephen. *The Existence and Attributes of God*. Minneapolis: Klock & Klock, 1977.
Congregational Praise. London: Independent Press for the Congregational Union of England and Wales, 1951.
Craig, William Lang. *Time and Eternity: Exploring God's Relationship to Time*. Wheaton: Crossway, 2001.
Cunningham, William. *Historical Theology*, 2 volumes. Edinburgh: Banner of Truth, 1960.
———. *The Reformers and the Theology of the Reformation*. London: Banner of Truth, 1967.
Dennison, James T. *The Market Day of the Soul*. Grand Rapids: Reformation Heritage Books, 2008.

Bibliography

Dolezal, James E. *All that is in God*. Grand Rapids: Reformation Heritage Books, 2017.

———. *God without Parts: Divine Simplicity and the Metaphysics of God's Absoluteness*. Eugene, OR: Pickwick, 2011.

Dressler, Harold H. P. "The Sabbath in the Old Testament." In *From Sabbath to Lord's Day*. Edited by D. A. Carson, 21–41. Eugene, OR: Wipf and Stock, 1999.

Edwards, Jonathan. *An Inquiry into the Freedom of the Will*. Morgan, PA: Soli Deo Gloria, 1996.

Fairbairn, Patrick. *The Revelation of Law in Scripture*. Phillipsburg, NJ: P&R, 1996.

———. *The Typology of Scripture*. Philadelphia: Smith & English, 1854.

Flew, Antony and Alasdair MacIntyre, eds. *New Essays in Philosophical Theology*. New York: Macmillan, 1964.

Frame, John M. *Apologetics to the Glory of God*. Phillipsburg; NJ: P&R, 1994.

———. *Cornelius Van Til: An Analysis of his Thought*. Phillipsburg, NJ: P&R, 1995.

———. *A History of Western Philosophy and Theology*. Phillipsburg, NJ: P&R, 2015.

Gaffin, Richard B., Jr. *Calvin and the Sabbath*. Fearn, Scotland: Christian Focus, 1998.

Harnack, Adolf. *History of Dogma*. 7 volumes. New York: Dover, 1951.

———. *Outlines of the History of Dogma*. Boston: Beacon, 1957.

Helm, Paul. *Eternal God: A Study of God without Time*. Oxford: Clarendon, 1988.

Hendriksen, William. *New Testament Commentary: Exposition of the Gospel According to John, Volume II*. Grand Rapids: Baker, 1954.

Hodge, A. A. *The Confession of Faith: A Handbook of Christian Doctrine Expounding the Westminster Confession*. London: Banner of Truth, 1958.

———. *Outlines of Theology*. Edinburgh: Banner of Truth, 1972.

Hodge, Charles. *Systematic Theology*. 3 volumes. London: Thomas Nelson, 1873.

Horton, Michael. *The Christian Faith: A Systematic Theology for Pilgrims On the Way*. Grand Rapids: Zondervan, 2011.

———. *Covenant and Salvation: Union with Christ*. Louisville: Westminster, 2007.

Howe, John. *The Works of the Reverend John Howe*. Three volumes. Ligonier, PA: Soli Deo Gloria, 1990.

Hughes, Philip Edgcumbe. *A Commentary on the Epistle to the Hebrews*. Grand Rapids: Eerdmans, 1977.

———. *Paul's Second Epistle to the Corinthians: The English text with introduction, exposition and notes*. Grand Rapids: Eerdmans, 1962.

Junius, Franciscus. *De theologue vera*. Translated by David C. Noe. In *A Treatise on True Theology with the Life of Franciscus Junius*. Grand Rapids: Reformation Heritage Books, 2014.

Kant, Immanuel. *Critique of Practical Reason*. Translated by Thomas Kingsmill Abbott. New York: Barnes & Noble, 2004.

———. *Critique of Pure Reason*. Translated by J. M. D. Meiklejohn. New York: Barnes & Noble, 2004.

Kelly, Douglas. *Systematic Theology: Grounded in Holy Scripture and understood in the light of the Church*. Fearn, Scotland: Mentor, 2008.

Krentz, Edgar. *The Historical-Critical Method*. Philadelphia: Fortress, 1975.

Luther, Martin. *A Commentary on St. Paul's Epistle to the Galatians*. Edited by Philip S. Watson. London: James Clarke, 1953.

Martin, Hugh. *The Abiding Presence*. Edinburgh: Knox, n.d.

McGraw, Ryan. *The Day of Worship: Reassessing the Christian life in the light of the Sabbath*. Grand Rapids: Reformation Heritage Books, 2011. Also ebooks edition.

Bibliography

———. *Knowing the Trinity*. Lancaster, PA: Alliance of Confessing Evangelicals, 2017.

———. Review of *Keeping the Sabbath Today*, by Jay E. Adams. *Puritan Reformed Journal* 1 (2009) 275-81.

McMillan, Duncan James and Alexander Jackson. *Sunday the World's Rest Day*. Garden City, NY: Doubleday, 1916.

Milton, John. *Paradise Lost*. In *The Norton Anthology of English Literature*, 452-547. Edited by M. H., Abrams, et al. New York: Norton, 1962.

Murray, John. *Collected Writings*. 4 volumes. Edinburgh: Banner of Truth, 1976-1982.

———. "Definitive sanctification." In *Collected Writings*, vol. 2, 277-84. Edinburgh: Banner of Truth, 1976-1982.

———. *The Epistle to the Romans: The English text with introduction, exposition and notes*, volume 1. Grand Rapids: Eerdmans, 1959.

———. *The Imputation of Adam's Sin*. Grand Rapids: Eerdmans, 1959.

———. *Principles of Conduct*. Grand Rapids: Eerdmans, 1957.

———. "Progressive Sanctification." In *Collected Writings*, vol. 2, 294-304. Edinburgh: Banner of Truth, 1976-1982.

———. *Redemption—Accomplished and Applied*. Grand Rapids: Eerdmans, 1955.

———. "The Sabbath Institution." In *Collected Writings*, vol. 1, 205-18. Edinburgh: Banner of Truth, 1976-1982.

Oliphint, K. Scott. *Covenantal Apologetics: Principles and Practice in Defense of Our Faith*. Wheaton, IL: Crossway, 2013.

Owen, John. "Of Communion with God the Father, Son, and Holy Spirit." In *The Works of John Owen*, vol. 2, 1-274. London: Banner of Truth, 1966.

Poole, Matthew. *A Commentary on the Holy Bible: Volume III: Matthew-Revelation*. London: Banner of Truth, 1963.

Ross, Philip S. *From the Finger of God: The Biblical and Theological Basis for the Threefold Division of the Law*. Fearn, Scotland: Mentor, 2010.

Savoy Declaration of Faith. Various editions.

Schleiermacher, Friedrich. *The Christian Faith*. Edinburgh: T. & T. Clark, 1928.

Second London (Baptist) Confession. Various editions.

Shedd, W. G. T. *A History of Christian Doctrine*. 2 volumes. New York: Scribner, 1868.

Smart, J. J. G. "The Existence of God." In *New Essays in Philosophical Theology*. Edited by Anthony Flew et al., 28-46. New York: Macmillan, 1964.

Sproul, R.C. *Faith Alone*. Grand Rapids: Baker, 1995.

Sproul, R. C., et al. *Classical Apologetics: A Rational Defense of the Christian Faith and a Critique of Presuppositional Apologetics*. Grand Rapids: Zondervan, 1984.

Stonehouse. N. B. and Paul Woolley, eds. *The Infallible Word: A symposium by the members of the faculty of Westminster Theological Seminary*. Grand Rapids: Eerdmans, 1946.

Thomas, W. H. Griffith. *The Principles of Theology: An Introduction to the Thirty-Nine Articles*. London: Church Book Room, 1951.

Tillich, Paul. *Systematic Theology*. Chicago: University of Chicago Press, 1952.

Trinity Hymnal. Atlanta: Great Commissions, 1990.

Turretin, F. *Institutes of Elenctic Theology, 3 Volumes*. Translated by George Musgrave Giger. Edited by James T. Dennison. Phillipsburg, NJ: P&R, 1992-1997.

Van Til, Cornelius. *A Christian Theory of Knowledge*. Philadelphia: Presbyterian and Reformed, 1969.

———. *Common Grace*. Philadelphia: Presbyterian and Reformed, 1954.

———. *The Defense of the Faith*. Philadelphia: Presbyterian and Reformed, 1963.

———. *The Defense of the Faith, Volume V, An Introduction to Systematic Theology.* Philadelphia: Presbyterian and Reformed, 1974.
———. *An Introduction to Systematic Theology.* Philadelphia: Presbyterian and Reformed, 1974.
———. "Nature and Scripture." In *The Infallible Word: A symposium by the members of the faculty of Westminster Theological Seminary.* Edited by N. B. Stonehouse, et al., 255–93. Grand Rapids: Eerdmans, 1946.
Vickers, Douglas. *Christian Confession and the Crackling Thorn.* Grand Rapids: Reformation Heritage Books, 2004.
———. *Discovering the Christian Mind.* Eugene, OR: Wipf & Stock, 2011.
———. *The Divine Purchase.* Eugene, OR: Wipf & Stock, 2016.
———. *Divine Redemption and the Refuge of Faith.* Grand Rapids: Reformation Heritage Books, 2005.
———. *The Immediacy of God.* Eugene, OR: Wipf & Stock, 2009.
———. *When God Converts a Sinner.* Eugene, OR: Wipf & Stock, 2008.
Vos, Geerhardus. *Biblical Theology: Old and New Testaments.* Grand Rapids: Eerdmans, 1959.
Waltke, Bruce. *Old Testament Theology: an exegetical, canonical, and thematic approach.* Grand Rapids: Zondervan, 2007.
Warfield, B. B. "The Foundations of the Sabbath in the Word of God." In Duncan James McMillan and Alexander Jackson, *Sunday the World's Rest Day*, 63–81. Garden City, NY: Doubleday, 1916.
Wellum, Stephen J. *God the Son Incarnate: The Doctrine of Christ.* Wheaton, IL: Crossway, 2016.
Westminster Confession of Faith. Various editions.
Westminster Larger Catechism. Various editions.
Westminster Shorter Catechism. Various editions.

www.ingramcontent.com/pod-product-compliance
Lightning Source LLC
Chambersburg PA
CBHW072151160426
43197CB00012B/2333